COOKOFFS!

COOKOFFS!

Including the blue-ribbon recipes from Texas' most famous food festivals.

ANN RUFF AND AUSTIN WEST

Copyright © 1986 by Ann Ruff and Austin West. All rights including reproduction by photographic or electronic process and translation into other languages are fully reserved under the International Copyright Union, the Universal Copyright Convention, and the Pan-American Copyright Convention. Reproduction or use of this book in whole or in part in any manner without written permission of the publisher is strictly prohibited.

Texas Monthly Press
P.O. Box 1569
Austin, Texas 78767

A B C D E F G H

Library of Congress Cataloging-in-Publication Data

Ruff, Ann, 1930–
   Cookoffs! : including blue ribbon recipes from Texas' most famous food festivals.

   1. Cookery, American—Southwestern style. 2. Cookery, American—Southwestern style—Competitions. 3. Texas—Social life and customs.
I. West, Austin. II. Title.
TX715.R9262   1986   641.59764   86-5994
ISBN 0-87719-056-9

Text design by Cathy Casey
Cover design by Hixo, Inc.

This book is dedicated to all those would-be cookoff champs who haven't yet earned a trophy. Keep on cooking!

CONTENTS

Introduction ... 1
FESTIVALS
Athens ... 3
Austin ... 7
Bertram and Oatmeal ... 9
Big Spring ... 11
Brady ... 13
Bryan ... 15
Caldwell ... 17
Carthage ... 19
Coleman ... 21
Copperas Cove ... 23
Cotulla ... 25
Edinburg ... 27
Fort Worth ... 29
Fredericksburg ... 31
Galveston ... 33
Gilmer ... 35
Hereford ... 37
Hondo ... 39
Laredo ... 41
Llano ... 43
Lufkin ... 45
Nixon ... 47
Noonday ... 49
Orange ... 51
Rosenburg ... 53
San Angelo ... 55
San Marcos ... 57
Stonewall ... 59
Sulphur Springs ... 61
Taylor ... 63
Terlingua ... 65
Wichita Falls ... 69
Winnie ... 71
Texas Chicken Cooking Contest ... 73
About Fajitas ... 75

Cookoffs!

RECIPES
    Soups, Salads, and Appetizers   77
    Vegetables and Pasta   89
    Bread   95
    Chili   111
    Meats and Main Courses   119
    Desserts and Pastries   153

Index   189

Introduction

Texans are by nature competitive folks, even though they can't all ride bulls or charge the Cowboys' defensive line. All Texans can eat, though, and most like to cook. Next to rodeo and football, food—the preparing and partaking thereof—might be the most favored pastime of Texans. We're talking, of course, about cookoffs and the people who follow them—those who compete and those who only stand and taste. A culture has evolved out of these weekend activities, many of which center on indigenous foods and dishes like chili, barbecue, black-eyed peas, yams, kolaches, and fajitas.

Practitioners of this pastime include first of all the cooks, both individuals and teams. Teams may consist of a husband and wife, two or three young men and their girl friends, members of a Lions Club or a Sunday school class, or a group from the local bank or hardware store. Teams give themselves more or less descriptive names (Conroe Corn Pones, Big Daddies From Decatur), purchase equipment including rolling stock like smokers on trailers, and build portable cases to display at the cook site the trophies they have won. They may participate in several cookoffs a season, or they may be specialists and enter only a particular event.

The typical cookoff scene varies little from place to place. The competitors arrive with an entourage of friends, family, and fol-

Cookoffs!

lowers who offer to help out—help drink the beer, help baste the ribs, help taste the chili. Meanwhile, artisans set up booths to show off their personalized Western belts, crocheted toilet-paper-roll covers, and native gemstone jewelry. Professional singers entertain at some events, sponsored perhaps by a radio station or brewery, and amplifiers fill the smoky air with the sounds of country tunes and twanging guitars. The people walking around wearing ribbons, distinctive caps, or aprons and observing the various cooking stations are the judges, who may include local entertainers, media celebrities, a bank president, and a politician or two.

Almost all cookoffs are for a good cause—good clean fun for the populace and sometimes a way to raise money for a worthy charity.

When you try these recipes, try to envision the air heavy with mesquite smoke, the voice of a country singer amplified across a country park, and onlookers cheering for a favorite team. It makes the food even better.

Besides cookoff recipes, we have included a few from a different type of competition—the county fair. These represent home cooking and canning, and they add variety to the usual round of fried, smoked, and grilled foods that you find at cookoffs.

We want to thank the cookoff sponsors and cooks for sharing their recipes with us. A few contests are not included in this book because the cooks are playing their recipe cards close to the apron, but other participants opened their recipe books and hearts to help us with this project, and to them we are grateful.

Athens

BLACK-EYED PEA JAMBOREE

Can you believe that Yankees consider black-eyed peas fit only for cattle fodder? Those Northerners have no concept that peas, pot liquor, and cornbread are food for the gods. The people of Athens, Texas, know how good peas are, though, and they also know how to stage a celebration: continuous live entertainment on the festival grounds, lots of games, the inevitable arts and crafts show, a pea-shelling contest (you need a really fast thumbnail to win this event), and a multitude of bad puns on the word "pea." The Black-eyed Pea Jamboree, which began modestly in 1970 on the courthouse square, is now world class, drawing entertainers such as Roy Clark, Waylon Jennings, and Willie Nelson.

All this razzmatazz is great fun, but the real nitty-gritty of the festival is the cookoff. It's hard to imagine that there could be any new recipes under the sun using black-eyed peas until you consider the prize-winning Pea-tini of some years back, which consisted of a very dry martini garnished with a black-eyed pea on a toothpick.

Contestants not only have to be creative with their reci-peas but they also must agree to stay up Saturday night and cook enough of their concoctions to feed five hundred people on Sunday. (At least

Cookoffs!

the Athens Chamber of Commerce supplies the ingredients.) The grand prize winner gets a purse of $900, which is not bad for a $12.50 entry-fee investment.

As is often the case in contests, some of the runner-up recipes are very complicated (such as the fantastic Pea-ta Bread Filled with Zucpea-ni Salad) while the grand champion winner (Black-eyed Peawheels) is marvelously simple.

**Third weekend July
Henderson County Fairgrounds
Athens Chamber of Commerce
P.O. Box 2600
Athens 75751
(214) 675-5181**

UNCLE FLETCH DAVIS MEMORIAL WORLD HAMBURGER COOKOFF

No less an authority than Hamburger University, the research organization of McDonald's, has declared that the hamburger was in all likelihood invented by an anonymous vendor at the St. Louis World's Fair in 1904—and no less an authority than the late Frank X. Tolbert, Texana connoisseur and columnist for the *Dallas Morning News*, subsequently declared that this anonymous inventor was in all probability one Fletcher Davis (1864–1941) of Athens, Texas.

According to his book *Tolbert's Texas*, a potter, odd-job man, and lunch-counter operator known affectionately as Old Dave was serving ground-beef sandwiches to the locals of Athens in the 1880s. John Murchison, a frequenter of Old Dave's little lunch counter on the Henderson County Courthouse Square, had vivid memories of the sandwich, which was classic in almost every way (served with a big slice of Bermuda onion, ground mustard mixed with mayonnaise, and sliced cucumber pickles), except that two slices of home-baked bread were used instead of today's ubiquitous bun.

Were it not for the world's fair, however, the hamburger would never have been more than a local delicacy or, for that matter, would never have received its name. When the fair opened, or soon after, Old Dave (who was from Missouri), went to St. Louis with his wife and started running a stand on the midway, where he served—what else—the ground-beef sandwiches that he invented at the cafe back home in Athens. A picture of him from this time, his identification portrait for the fair, shows a neatly dressed man of early middle age with shaggy hair, eyebrows that meet over his nose, and a real soup-strainer of a moustache. A *New York Tribune* writer reporting on the fair wrote that a new sandwich called a hamburger was "the innovation of a food vendor on the pike" (pike meant midway). The reporter also asked the sandwich vendor (whom he did not identify by name, unfortunately) about the fried potatoes he was serving. Apparently Old Dave had learned to cook them that way from a friend in Paris, Texas, but the reporter misunderstood and wrote that they were "french fried potatoes." If this is to be taken at face value, Old Dave should be given credit not only for the hamburger but also for the french fry.

As for the origin of the name "hamburger," it is probably lost to history. At this point, at least, there is only speculation. James A. Cockrell, a longtime editor of the St. Louis *Globe-Democrat*, told *Dallas News* columnist Tolbert that in his opinion the name was essentially an ethnic "in" joke. The city had at the time a large German population, and those originally from the southern part of that country had considerable scorn for those from the north; they coupled this dislike with a double helping of disdain for the residents of the northern city of Hamburg, who were traditionally very fond of ground meat. Thus, they dubbed Old Dave's sandwiches "hamburgers." It's an intriguing theory, in any case.

When the fair was over, Old Dave returned to Athens and went back to making pottery. He didn't reopen his lunch counter, though he would sometimes cook hamburgers at picnics. He was proud of his invention but he was not the kind of man who would ever have thought of commercializing it.

A historic note: When the Athens Chamber of Commerce held the second hamburger cookoff in 1985, the winner in the professional category was David Knouse, a co-owner of Tolbert's Texas

Cookoffs!

Chili Parlor in Dallas. The parlor, as you might guess, was started by indefatigable hamburger researcher Frank X. Tolbert.

**First held in 1984 but suspended
for the time being
Athens Chamber of Commerce
P.O. Box 2600
Athens 75751
(214) 675-5181**

Austin

TEXAS ICE CREAM CRANK-OFF

Imagine a bright June Saturday in Austin—clear blue skies, gentle breezes, and temperatures stretching toward but not quite reaching the critical mark that relegates outdoor recreation to the vicinity of a swimming pool. Now who wants to spend this glorious day downtown?

Ice cream lovers might, if it is the Saturday of the state ice cream crank-off on the state Capitol grounds. The contest draws finalists from across the state, who come to prove that Texas products make the best ice cream. All flavoring ingredients (except vanilla and chocolate) must be from Texas, but that leaves a broad field. Entries in the 1985 crank-off featured Texas strawberries, peaches, peanuts, sweet potatoes, and even jalapeños and cottonseeds.

Recipes for entries must be typed or printed on an index card and mailed to the Texas Department of Agriculture before the middle of May each year. A board of ice cream lovers from the department

Cookoffs!

and experts from Texas A&M University select the finalists. Shrimp sherbet, anyone? Pinto parfait?

A Saturday in June, may be suspended in 1987
State Capitol grounds
Eleventh Street and Congress Avenue
Texas Department of Agriculture
P.O. Box 12847
Austin 78711
(512) 463–7565

Bertram and Oatmeal

OATMEAL FESTIVAL

If you really want to feel your oats, spend Labor Day weekend at the Oatmeal Festival in Bertram. It's held in Bertram, incidentally, because there is nothing left at the site of the community of Oatmeal (so called for a German family named Habermill, or Oatmeal) except an ancient school building. Actually, there's not that much at Bertram either, but you can find it on a Texas highway map, between Burnet and Georgetown on Texas Highway 29. Oatmeal is due south. The festival originated in 1978 when the Texas Highway Department announced it was taking Oatmeal off the official travel map. In protest against such flaky behavior, the Oatmeal Festival was born.

The activities begin on Friday night at the rickety old school in Oatmeal with a barbecue well attended by local folks. Afterward, the younger crowd stages contests for Little Miss Oatmeal Cookie, Ms. Bag of Oats, and Mr. Groaty Oats. Saturday is the big day, with the festivities held in "beautiful downtown Bertram." Among other things, participants can try their hands at stacking oatmeal boxes supplied by the National Oats Company. Because the festival as a whole is sponsored by the makers of 3-Minute Oats, all contests begin at three minutes past the hour. The tastiest part is the oatmeal

Cookoffs!

cookoff, in which you'll see more inspired uses for oats than you ever dreamed possible. Oatmeal is definitely back on the map.

**Labor Day Weekend
Chamber of Commerce
Bertram 78605
(512) 355-2197**

Big Spring

CHICKEN-FRIED STEAK WORLD CHAMPIONSHIP

People who didn't grow up in Texas believe that chicken-fried steak is a put-on, like those jackalope trophies you see in roadside souvenir shops.

Gary Cartwright, *Texas Monthly*, February 1983

Judging from the number of chili cookoffs, a lot of people obviously agree that chili is rightfully the official state dish of Texas. But a large contingent, who have cream gravy in their veins, are equally convinced that the *real* test of downhome Texas cooking is the chicken-fried steak, or CFS.

Reduced to its essence, a chicken-fried steak is a tough, no-account piece of meat that has been tenderized, floured or battered, and then fried, chicken-style. Traditionally, it is topped with a "cream" gravy made from the pan drippings, a little flour, and milk. CFS is simple, quick, and cheap. And it's the most ubiquitous cafe food in Texas, with the possible exception of enchiladas.

The alleged First Ever Chicken-fried Steak World Championship

Cookoffs!

was held in Big Spring in 1985, when Dave Wrinkle of radio station KBST won the grand prize. He said that he had to come up with a surefire trick to insure that the judges would remember his creation, so he marinated the meat in fiery jalapeño juice. He must have succeeded; his entry beat out thirty-eight others.

Second weekend in October
Highland Mall, FM Road 700 and U.S. Highway 87
Dave Wrinkle Station KBST
P.O. Box 1632
Big Spring 79721–1632
(915) 267–6391

Brady
GOAT COOKOFF

When you attend the giant goat gala in Brady, you'll be right in the middle of things in Texas—literally. Brady is only a hop, skip, and a bleat from the geographic center of the Lone Star State. The McCulloch County Courthouse has a weather vane with a big red heart on the cupola, and on the lawn is another large heart carved from granite. The citizens of Brady take seriously this business of being deep in the heart of Texas.

Contest entrants work hard to see that the judges "get their goat." If you don't get to sample the prize-winning recipe, there is still plenty of barbecued goat to be had, served up with all the trimmings by the local chamber of commerce. Afterward, try your hand at milking one of the nannies or test your skill at the goat-pill flip. (A goat pill is the goat counterpart of the cow patty.)

Cookoffs!

In 1985, a trio from Llano—Richard Jackson, Ezra Horton, and Ronnie Horton—beat out 124 other entries to win the grand championship trophy.

Saturday of Labor Day weekend
Chamber of Commerce
101 East First Street
Brady 76825
(915) 597-2420

Bryan
MESSINA HOF WINEFEST

Texas vineyards are beginning to produce wines that can, in some instances, compete with the best California has to offer, proving that the Lone Star State can be famous for something other than cattle, oil, and Southfork. While the Panhandle, the Hill Country, and the Trans-Pecos are all promising vine-growing areas, one of the best is located just outside Bryan, and it is being developed by Messina Hof.

This winery was born on May 5, 1977, with the marriage of Paul and Merrill Bonarrigo. Messina, Sicily, was the home of Paul's family and Hof, Germany, was the home of Merrill's. Through their combined efforts, more than thirty acres of grapes are being cultivated to produce award-winning wines. One of the wines is a full-bodied port with smooth, rich complexity.

The Messina Hof family represents six generations of wine makers, and in the Messina family, the eldest son is always named Paul. One tradition that this generation has instituted is a spring festival at the winery. Other than sampling the wines, the festivities include a

Cookoffs!

pie-baking contest, with categories for cream, pecan, and fruit pies. Joan McDonald's Rum Cream Pie won first place in 1985.

Third weekend in April
Merrill Bonarrigo
Route 7
Box 905
Bryan 77802
(409) 779-2411

Caldwell
KOLACHE FESTIVAL

Caldwell's fall festival honors the kolache (usually pronounced ko-*lah*-chee in Texas), the original Czech wedding pastry. Celebrants have a chance to sample and take home a variety of these sweets, and they can also watch expert cooks divulge their special techniques.

Around the courthouse square, local organizations and artists set up display booths offering wood carvings, dolls, crochet work, belt buckles, and Christmas decorations. Visitors stroll among them to the tones of an antique dulcimer. While they're shopping, admiring the collections of Czech lead crystal, and learning how to decorate Czech Easter eggs, a jury of kolache tasters is hard at work in the courthouse, sampling the various entries—poppy seed, cheese, peach, sausage. Visitors can stop for lemonade, hand-cranked ice cream, fajitas wrapped in a warm tortilla, or hot sausage, then gather with the crowd at noon for the announcement of the new Burleson County kolache champion.

The Czechs have a saying: "Without work, there are no kolaches." Are they worth it? Ask Ella Drgac of Caldwell, who got up at four in the morning to start the kolaches that won the 1985 championship, or Mary Siptak, whose peach-filled pastries came in

Cookoffs! a close second. She's been making kolaches for seventy-five of her eighty-two years.

**Second weekend in September
Courthouse square, downtown Caldwell
Chamber of Commerce
Box 126
Caldwell 77836
(409) 567–7979**

Carthage
POTLATCH

Among the Indians of the Northwest Coast of the United States, a ceremony known as a potlatch was held when a young man assumed his rightful status in society. To fete the guests, lavish feasts were held and gifts of great value were recklessly distributed, frequently resulting in the giver having to declare the Indian equivalent of Chapter 11. As is true today, however, no stigma attached to this, and the gift giver was seen as someone more to be envied than pitied.

The people of Panola County (the name comes from *panolo*, meaning "cotton") today stage their own version of a potlatch celebration. You can acquire gifts (though you have to give something to the arts and crafts vendors in return) and you can observe the world's corniest cookoff. Some people might say, "Shucks, how

Cookoffs!

many ways can you cook corn?" But the first time the cookoff was held, fifty-seven recipes were submitted.

**Third week in October
Panola County Chamber of Commerce
P.O. Box 207
Carthage 75633
(214) 693-6634**

Coleman

FIESTA DE LA PALOMA AND DOVE COOKOFF

Coleman is in one of the largest dove-hunting regions of Texas, and the dove cookoff gives cooks a chance to show how delicious these little critters can be. The rules specify that the doves used in the cookoff must come from the local area. Usually about forty cooks enter; the male contestants lean toward barbecuing while the female participants devise more exotic combinations. The woman who wone the 1985 contest used a recipe that had proved its worth by winning two previous dove cookoffs.

The Fiesta de la Paloma gives the whole town a good excuse to turn out. The show barns on the rodeo grounds hold exhibits of antiques, needlework, and home-canned foods, while other areas in the arena host the arts and crafts show, flea market, and commercial booths. A dance caps off the day and everyone goes home happy—no one more so than the winner of the dove cookoff. In

Cookoffs!

1985 the winner garnered a trip to San Francisco, while in 1984 the prize included a trip to Cancún, Mexico.

A Saturday in late September
Coleman Rodeo Grounds
Coleman Chamber of Commerce
Box 796
Coleman 76834
(915) 625–2163

Copperas Cove

RABBIT FEST

In Copperas Cove, when you hear people talking about their Palominos, Angoras, or Lilacs, they aren't necessarily discussing horses, goats, or flowers. They could be discussing rabbits. In this city, Peter Cottontail has company in the form of Silver Martens, Rexes, Flemish Giants, Dwarf Hotots, and Florida Whites. Talk about splitting hares.

At Rabbit Fest each May, you can see all these bunnies and more at the civic center. Behind some thousand twitching noses are rabbits as large as a small dog and as small as a rat. Not all of their ears stand up like Bugs Bunny's, either. Some flop and others lie straight back.

A show-class rabbit must have a tattoo in its ear indicating its pedigree. All its toenails have to be the same color, eyes the same shade, no abnormal overbite (presumably buck teeth are allowed), and of course its coat has to be worthy of a Neiman-Marcus label. Good manners count. A rabbit that tries to run away from the judging table may be disqualified. On the other hand, if it relaxes and stretches out, it loses points too. A well-behaved bunny hunkers down and stays put.

Meanwhile, out on the fairgrounds a group of cooks is hopping

Cookoffs!

around, cooking up some out-of-the-ordinary dishes with rabbit as the main ingredient. No, the losers from the civic center don't end up on the grill. Commercially dressed rabbits are used for this, although it was hard recently to find enough for the 1985 contestants to stew, bake, and barbecue. Not surprisingly, the barbecued bunny won.

First weekend in May
Copperas Cove Chamber of Commerce
311 South First Street
Copperas Cove 76522
(817) 547–7416

Cotulla

LA SALLE COUNTY WILD HOG COOKOFF

The wild hog cookoff began in 1980 when the La Salle County Fair Association was squealing for funds to improve the fairgrounds. Other cities had cornered the market on chili and fajitas, but the citizens of Cotulla realized they had a prime untapped natural resource in the thousands of feral hogs that run wild in the brush. Descended from domestic hogs, these animals are a nuisance to local ranchers and are hunted year round.

The obvious solution to the twin problems of raising money to improve the fairgrounds and reducing the hog population was to make the hogs the center of Cotulla's own cookoff. This soon happened, and while the fair association isn't exactly wallowing in money yet, it's on its way.

First weekend in March
Linda Oltmann
Route 1
Box 81
Cotulla 78014
(512) 879–2844

Edinburg

PANOCHA BREAD COOKOFF

Panocha is a type of skillet bread that is cooked over an open campfire, and though its origin and the meaning of its peculiar name are buried in time, there's still a touch of Western romance about it.

Did cowboys eat panocha? More to the point, did they name it? One dictionary of Spanish words describes panocha as a kind of tamal (or "tamale" in Tex-Mex usage). Another source suggests panocha is a variation of "panela", or "piloncillo", referring to the syrup extracted from raw sugar cane. To Spanish-speaking cowboys, panocha is a special bread, much bigger and thicker than a tortilla. To us today, it's a bread to whip up for camp-outs or any time that we want to imagine what life on the trail might have been like.

Look at a Texas road map and you will see that U.S. Highway 281 follows a direct north-south route from the Rio Grande Valley to the Red River. Roughly a century ago this was the Chisholm Trail, and many a cowboy rode behind a herd of bawling Longhorns up this trail to the railhead in Kansas. Some historians claim that here in the *brasada*, or brush country, of South Texas, the cowboy was born.

Cookoffs!

First Saturday in November; rain date, second Saturday
Thomas Esparza
811 South Sixteenth Avenue
Edinburg 78539
(512) 383—2285 or 383—1182

Fort Worth

PIONEER DAYS FAJITA COOKOFF

The Pioneer Days festival commemorates the era of the big cattle drives, when Fort Worth was a rip-snorting, hell-raising stop on the Chisholm Trail. When the Texas and Pacific Railroad reached Fort Worth in 1876, the city snapped to attention, organized stockyards, and by 1878 had shipped over 2200 rail cars of cattle. Meat packing grew to be an important industry. Tiny Niles City, a community of 650 located where the stockyards are today, in 1922 had more millionaires per capita than any other place in the country.

Although it seems as though Fort Worth has always been Cowtown, there was a time when it looked as if the stockyards would be demolished. Fortunately, a group of dedicated citizens managed to get the entire area entered on the National Register of Historic Places. It has been preserved ever since and, indeed, is one of the biggest tourist attractions in the city. It is the logical location for celebrations with a Western flavor, and one of the best is Pioneer Days, every September, with music, food, dramatized shoot-outs, and a gentle Longhorn that obligingly allows its photograph to be taken

Cookoffs!

with tourists posed precariously on its back. The fajita cookoff, naturally, is a highlight.

**Third weekend in September
Kearley & Company
222 West Exchange
Fort Worth 76106
(817) 625–6349**

Fredericksburg

GILLESPIE COUNTY FAIR

Visitors to Fredericksburg today are enchanted by its retention of the flavor of its German past. The city was founded on May 8, 1846, by immigrants led by John O. Meusebach, a baron in his former country. Meusebach here signed a famous treaty with the Comanches, which was broken by neither side, although other Indian treaties were violated with regularity.

This orderly and pacific past is evident in Fredericksburg today. Main Street is broad and clean, lined with quaint gift and antique shops; numerous houses of the nineteenth century have been restored and are open to the public on various festival days or have been turned into charming bed-and-breakfast inns. Fredericksburg is unique in Texas for its Sunday houses, diminutive, Munchkinland houses built as weekend residences. Rather than make two arduous treks to town on Saturday for market day and again on Sunday for church, the early farmers constructed these small townhouses so their families could stay overnight.

The Gillespie County Fair draws on this abundant heritage and Germans' love of good food. Pickles, jellies, jams, canned goods,

Cookoffs! cakes, and cookies are entered, as are examples of handwork, sewing, quilting, and other crafts. There are also horse races, a carnival, refreshments, and dances in the evening in an outdoor pavilion.

**Third weekend in August
Gillespie County Fairgrounds, Texas Highway 16
Fredericksburg Chamber of Commerce
P.O. Box 506
Fredericksburg 78624
(512) 997-6523**

Galveston

ICE CREAM CRANK-OFF AT ASHTON VILLA

For the past ten years, the charming Victorian mansion known as Ashton Villa has opened its gates wide for a Fourth of July Family Picnic and Ice Cream Crank-off. Visitors are encouraged to bring their children, a blanket, and a picnic lunch. Those who find a picnic basket too much trouble can partake of the hot dogs, lemonade, and champagne for sale on the grounds. Dessert is always the same—homemade ice cream. After the judges have finished tasting the efforts of the fifteen or so finalists, the contents of the freezers are offered to the picnickers.

If you can't make it to Galveston for the Fourth, don't fret. The ice cream may not be there when you do arrive, but the villa will. It may be seen on guided tours sponsored by the Galveston Historical Foundation, which maintains and occupies the building. It was built in 1859, during the era of Galveston's heyday as a port and the

Cookoffs!

leading city of Texas, and it is one of the must-see attractions on any tour of the city.

Fourth of July
Ashton Villa Grounds, 2328 Broadway
Betty Massey
Ashton Villa
P.O. Box 1616,
Galveston 77553
(409) 762-3933

Gilmer

THE YAMBOREE

Back in 1935 Upshur County had one of the few weevil-free yam crops in Texas. The farmers decided to celebrate, and the Yamboree was born. Fifty years later, Gilmer, with a population of sixty-four-hundred, hosted some fifty thousand people for the forty-eighth annual Yamboree (World War II caused the cancellation of a few Yamborees in the forties).

Yams aren't the big crop around Gilmer anymore; dairy and beef cattle, other agriculture, and some small industries have surpassed the yam on the local economic scene. But the Yamboree endures. If you want yams, go to Daingerfield. If you want an outstanding fall festival, come to Gilmer.

The Yamboree serves as a sort of county fair, with a livestock show, craft and hobby exhibits, canning contests, a carnival, an old-time fiddlers' contest, two parades, a barn dance, and continuous music from two bandstands.

Now we're going to let you in on a secret. Carolyn Bassham of Gilmer has devised the most delicious yam pie that one lifelong devotee has ever put to his lips (no small claim considering that this person has tasted the best pies that Texas and Georgia yams have

Cookoffs!

to offer). It won the Yamboree Yam Pie Cookoff, and if there were an award for best in book, it would probably take the blue ribbon.

Third weekend in October
Yamboree grounds, U.S. Highway 271 North;
and the Upshur County Courthouse Square
June Johnson
Upshur County Chamber of Commerce
P.O. Box 854
Gilmer 75644
(214) 843-2413

Hereford

NATIONAL COWGIRL HALL OF FAME CHILI COOKOFF

In the heart of Texas cow country, Hereford is just a few miles from neighboring New Mexico. Here, in an annual summer contest, women compete in most of the same rodeo events that men do elsewhere: they ride bareback broncs, bulls, and steers; do team and calf roping; and "undecorate" a running steer, which consists of removing a ribbon taped to the animal's back. The most popular event is barrel racing, which tests riding skill and speed as the cowgirls do a kind of slalom on horseback around barrels spaced about a course.

Women who have done much to promote the Western tradition of the rodeo are inducted each year into the Cowgirl Hall of Fame. Not all inductees ride the rodeo circuit, for this museum honors the spirit and strength of the Western woman and numbers among its members Henrietta King, matriarch of the King Ranch; Louise Massey, composer of "My Adobe Hacienda"; and Margaret Harper, who helped create the pageant "Texas."

Like all museums, the Cowgirl Hall of Fame feels the constant need of funds to maintain its building and add to the exhibits. The

Cookoffs!

chili cookoff is its answer to this problem; proceeds benefit the museum. In 1985, Richard Forrest, an attorney in Hereford, won the People's Choice trophy with an unusual recipe showing a strong New Mexico influence in the use of green chiles and green tomatoes.

Second weekend in July
National Cowgirl Hall of Fame
P.O. Box 1742
Hereford 79045
(806) 364–5252

Hondo

WINTER GARDEN PECAN BAKE SHOW

Several counties in the South Texas farming region—east of the state's desert areas—have been lumped together under the appellation Winter Garden. Frio, Uvalde, Dimmit, Medina, Val Verde, and Maverick counties, known for winter vegetables, at one time sponsored jointly a winter pecan show that always included examples of the most delightful ways to cook and serve pecans.

Now that many of the counties have their own shows, the Medina County Extension Homemakers Council and the Texas Agricultural Extension Service sponsor the Winter Garden Pecan Show in Hondo, one of the state's prime pecan-growing areas.

There are no restrictions on entries for the pecan judging; they can come from anywhere in the state. Each year, some three hundred to five hundred pecan growers enter their choice pecans, to be judged by quality. The horticultural varieties bearing Indian names, such as the Tejas and the Choctaw, predominate.

The bake show attracts more than one hundred entries from as far away as Carrizo Springs and Eagle Pass, and winners go on to regional and state competitions. Judging by the entries we have

Cookoffs!

tried, the winners at Hondo are good enough for any size of contest.

Incidentally, the folks at Hondo have proof that the neighborhood has been a garden area for quite a while. In Hondo Creek are the easily discernible tracks of the forty-foot-long, fifteen-ton herbivorous dinosaurs belonging to the genus *Trachodon*. Look for the tracks in the creek, twenty-three miles north of Hondo off FM Road 462.

**First week in December
Medina County Fairgrounds
Gaye Bippert, County Extension Agent
1312 Avenue K
Hondo 78861
(512) 426-2233**

Laredo
JALAPEÑO FESTIVAL

Jalapeño burgers! Jalapeño cornbread! Stuffed jalapeños! Texans love these incendiary green peppers, and some hardy souls will eat them alongside almost anything. The jalapeño-eating contest (a masochistic form of self-expression at best) is a mainstay of many a Texas festival, including this one, the Washington's Birthday Celebration held every year in Laredo.

This admittedly peculiar celebration came about some years ago when the Fraternal Order of the Redman wished to stage an event that would unite the two sides of the border. Since both the United States and Mexico honor George Washington, his birthday was chosen as the focus of the festivities. It has become Laredo's own Mardi Gras, with two parades, fireworks, the Colonial Pageant and Ball (a debutante affair), and Noche Mexicana (a Mexican-style variety show). One of the more amusing events is the International Waiters Race, in which agile *mozos* try to carry a tray bearing a bottle and glass of champagne across a finish line without spilling a drop.

Cookoffs!

The Jalapeño Festival includes both a jalapeño-eating contest and a jalapeño-foods cookoff.

**Saturday nearest February 22
Jarvis Plaza, Matamoros and Salinas Streets,
Downtown
Washington's Birthday Association
P.O. Box 816
Laredo 78042
(512) 722-0589**

Llano

WILD GAME COOKOFF

When you drive through Llano today, it is hard to realize that around the turn of the century this small ranching town on the fringe of the Hill Country was a boomtown bursting with thirty thousand people. Most were the dupes of speculators, unfortunately, who declared that gold, silver, and every other mineral under the sun could be found in the geological formation known as the Llano Uplift. The boom fizzled, though, and all that was left was the granite that had been there originally, enough to stock every graveyard in the United States. Llano became known as the Tombstone of the Southwest.

Not much has happened in Llano since that exciting era, and the town spends most of the year waiting for April and November, when it comes alive again. April is glorious, with millions of bluebonnets, and November marks the start of hunting season, which is the excuse for the Wild Game Cookoff. Llano's present and better-deserved sobriquet is the Deer Capital of the World.

The game cookoff is part of the Black-Powder Shoot, among other things a costume party with plenty of fringe, coonskin caps, and buckskin. Contestants enter game recipes and also some for tamer goat, beef, poultry, and pork. The winner in 1985, Les Inman of Llano, made a unique barbecue sauce without tomatoes. (Maybe

Cookoffs!

next year the contest organizers will have a competition to decide what you call natives of Llano. Llanolians?)

**First weekend in November
Llano Chamber of Commerce
700 Bessemer
Llano 78643
(915) 247–5354**

Lufkin

SOUTHERN HUSHPUPPY OLYMPICS

Texas' wealth has become so synonymous with oil and cattle that it is hard to realize that at one time, big bucks were made in lumber. The people around Lufkin, in the heart of the East Texas Piney Woods, still produce a million board feet a year, and they haven't forgotten the debt Texas owes its forests. Fittingly, the Texas Forestry Association established a museum honoring Texas trees and the lumbering industry. You can visit it at 1905 Atkinson Drive.

Each spring the community of Lufkin stages a Forestry Festival, where lumberjacks clad in traditional woolen pants, plaid shirts, and brightly colored suspenders participate in events such as the eighty-foot pole climb, tree chopping, and logrolling. You halfway expect Paul Bunyan and Babe the Blue Ox to show up.

The Hoo-Hoo Band concert is another part of the Forestry Festival. For those of you not in the know, a hoo-hoo is the tuft of hair on a bald man's head. In 1904 the Concatenated Order of the Hoo-Hoo and the Lufkin Trib Band performed at the Hoo-Hoo Convention at the World's Fair in St. Louis, but to achieve this honor, the Trib

Cookoffs!

Band had to change its name to that of the Hoo. Today the hoo-hoos have been reborn, complete with replicas of the original uniforms, under the directorship of Glenn Miller (no, not *that* Glenn Miller). Members are no longer required to have hoo-hoos and, in a major concession to the twentieth century, women are allowed to join.

The winner of the Southern Hushpuppy Olympics for three years, was seventy-year-old-plus O. O. ("Shotgun") Wright, who always makes sure that his hushpuppies don't fade into the crowd, by craftily molding them in the shape of the judges' initials.

Third weekend in May
Angelina County Chamber of Commerce
Southern Hushpuppy Olympics
P.O. Box 1606
Lufkin 75901
(409) 634−6644

Nixon

FEATHER FEST

The fact that Gonzales County is the state's largest producer of poultry-related items is not a statistic that is bandied about the national media. Nevertheless, the residents of Nixon know the source of their golden eggs and they get themselves into a truly fowl mood on Labor Day each year for the occasion of the annual Feather Fest.

Citizens hope to earn enough butter-and-egg money from the celebration to build a community center in the not-too-distant future. In the meantime, the chicken-cooking contest is the primary source of the growing nest egg of the Feather Fest.

Labor Day
Nixon Chamber of Commerce
104 North Texas Avenue
Nixon 78140
(512) 582–1711

Noonday
ONION FESTIVAL

Noonday (population: 56), located five miles from Tyler in Northeast Texas, has one claim to fame: its very own variety of onion. Like the Vidalia onion that is exported in quantity from the town of the same name in Georgia, the hybrid Noonday onion tastes particularly good because of some indefinable quality of the soil or factor in the climate here, or perhaps a combination of the two.

    The Noonday onion was originally developed to the specifications of a local farmer, and now all the farmers around this small Smith County community grow the Noonday, right along with the roses for which the Tyler area is famous. Although folks here say that the Noonday is even more delicious than the Vidalia, its high moisture content means that it doesn't travel well. Most of the growers sell to regular customers, who arrive every year in early summer to buy onions by the bushel. The rest of the harvest is sold from roadside stands and off pickup trucks to onion cognoscenti from Dallas to Shreveport. You won't find the Noonday in grocery stores.

    What's so great about Noonday onions? According to cookoff winner Diane Smotherman, "They don't have a bite and they are very sweet. You can eat them like apples." She devises recipes to

Cookoffs!

take advantage of this, including her grand-prize recipe for Onion Praline Ice Cream.

**A Saturday in May, to be announced
Noonday United Methodist Church
Claudia Jackson (214) 561–6918
or Beverly Mason 894–6602**

Orange
INTERNATIONAL GUMBO COOKOFF

Longfellow didn't know about it when he wrote "Evangeline," but some of the French Canadians, or Cajuns, who settled Louisiana kept on going west and found themselves in Texas. Thus, traditional cajun gumbo is equally indigenous to the Lone Star State.

As much as they like food, Cajuns like music, and the International Gumbo Cookoff starts with a street dance on Friday night and continues with live music all day Saturday. Most of the contestants are from either Texas or Louisiana, though some come from far parts of the country. (Of course, the natives have a built-in advantage in that they're born with wooden spoons in their hands—the better for stirring the roux.)

The various classes of gumbo in the cookoff include *poisson* (made with fish or seafood), *gibier* (game), and a combination of shrimp, chicken, and sausage gumbo. Reporters and writers can enter the media contest (the *Orange Leader* team regularly scores).

Contestants simmer their gumbos in twenty-gallon cauldrons. They are allowed to prepare the vegetables ahead of time but they must make the roux at the cookoff site. Once the judges have finished evaluating the entries, the cooks are free to sell whatever is

Cookoffs!

left over. Considering how much effort goes into making a good gumbo, buying a quart or so for dinner seems like an excellent idea.

First weekend in May
Old Naval Base, Simmons Drive
Joseph Anderson
Greater Orange Chamber of Commerce
P.O. Box 218
Orange, 77630
(409) 883-3536

Rosenberg

FORT BEND COUNTY CZECH FEST

When General Sam Houston led the motley Texas army in its confrontation with the forces of Mexican leader Santa Anna at the climax of the Texas Revolution in 1836, a young Czech lad, Frederick Lemsky, signaled the attack, playing on his fife a popular romantic tune of the day, "Will You Come to the Bower?" The Battle of San Jacinto, which took place on the Coastal Plains not so terribly far from Fort Bend County, determined Texas' destiny as first a republic and then a state.

Today, Czech Texans retain their ethnic identity and share their heritage with others at occasions like the Fort Bend County Czech Fest. Generous helpings of music and what amounts to the Czech national dish—the kolache, a type of fruit-filled pastry—bring as many as sixty thousand souls to this annual festival, held since 1976. The first festival brought out enough hungry folks to wolf down in two hours the five-hundred-dozen kolaches that local cooks had prepared for the three-day event.

They've learned, those Czechs, that hungry hordes from Austin, Houston, and points in between will descend on their peaceful community on the first weekend in May, and now they are prepared not

Cookoffs!

only with kolaches but also with *bramborové placky* (potato pancakes), *klobásy* (sausage), sauerkraut, and most especially *klobásníky* (foot-long sausages encased in kolache dough).

The Czech Texans of Fort Bend County are descendants of workers who came to build the railroad west from Galveston. After they completed the line through the county, many of the laborers decided to settle on the inviting farmland. At the festival, modern Czechs celebrate their heritage, arts and crafts, music, and cuisine. The kolache bake-off on Saturday morning brings out some of the best cooks in Southeast Texas, and some of the best eaters, too.

First full weekend in May
Fort Bend County Fairgrounds
Margaret Oldmixon
Rosenberg/Richmond Area Chamber of Commerce
4120 Avenue H
Rosenberg 77471
(713) 342—5465

San Angelo

ARMED FORCES ANNUAL CHILI COOKOFF

Most Texas chili cookoffs are open to just about anyone with the entry fee and a cast-iron palate. Entrants don't even have to be Texans, though you can easily spot out-of-state chili because it tends to have unsanctioned ingredients such as celery, tomatoes, and—the biggest no-no of all—beans. Texans don't care too much what you add in the way of spices, and the meat can be anything from armadillo to rattlesnake, but if you cook beans *with* the meat you'll never win a chili cookoff in Texas.

The Armed Forces Annual Chili Cookoff in San Angelo draws participants from all over the country; entrants have to be either active or retired members of the armed forces. One reward for winning is that the champion is automatically qualified to compete for the World Championship in Terlingua without having to accumulate more points. The logic is that members of the armed services have more important things to do than spend spare weekends attending chili cookoffs.

The armed forces cookoff chili that went to Terlingua in 1985 was Bill and Janie Mohler's "Old Snort" Chili. Bill explained, "I had a horse one time—*mean*—and I named him Old Snort because all

Cookoffs!

he would do was snort and pitch." (Don't think too hard about what that has to do with the chili.)

**First weekend after Labor Day
San Angelo Chili Society
Goodfellow Technical Training Center
3480 Air Base Group/CC
Goodfellow Air Force Base 76908–5000
(915) 657–3407**

LAMBLAST

Let's face it. Texas is famous for its cattle. (Whoever heard of heading 'em up and moving 'em out with a herd of sheep?) But in San Angelo, sheep ranchers have a different attitude toward the woolly critters, and this area claims to be the Wool Capital of the World.

To spread the word to beef-loving Texans that lamb is not only edible but delicious, a group of San Angeloans and cartoonist Ace Reid came up with the idea of staging a lamb cookoff in 1977. A lot of good and a few b-a-a-a-d suggestions for a name for the event were offered, and it almost became the Lamb-a-Rama. "Lamblast" won out, and when the first cookoff was held in 1978, it lived up to its name—and it still does.

**Third Saturday in April
Ross McSwain
San Angelo *Standard Times*
P.O. Box 511
San Angelo 76902
(915) 653–1221**

San Marcos

REPUBLIC OF TEXAS CHILYMPIAD

The temperature is still mighty hot in Texas in September, and so is the chili in San Marcos. What else would you expect with four hundred pots simmering away? When San Marcos hosts the Republic of Texas Chilympiad, there is a hot time in the old town in more ways than one. Over a period of four days, which are liberally sprinkled with fun and entertainment, cooks vie to win the coveted honor of being the best chili chef in Texas.

One aspect of this competition that bears close scrutiny by supporters of women's rights is that the contest is open to men only. The late, great chili-history chronicler Frank X. Tolbert traced the origin of this rule to Harold Robbins' comment, "No woman is qualified to cook chili." Being one of the founding fathers of the chilympiad, Robbins saw to it that his controversial dictum became law. Naturally, many chili-libbers have raised their voices and cooking spoons in protest, but the chili chauvinists remain in force. Until the time that women are allowed to enter the chilympiad, a man is always destined to be the state champion chili cook.

In 1985 Tom Tyler of Mesquite won the contest with his North Texas Red Chili. Even though his wife Linda Tyler is an equal partner

Cookoffs!

and has been a co-winner of over two hundred chili trophies, she remains unacknowledged because of the anachronistic rules of the chilympiad. Let's hear it for Linda Tyler!

Third weekend in September
Pat Murdock
Southwest Texas State University
San Marcos 78666–4613
(512) 245–2180

Stonewall

PEACH JAMBOREE

The famous Texas Stonewall peaches owe their origin to Joseph W. Stubenrauch, a native of Bavaria who settled near the Texas town of Mexia in 1877. The so-called Peach Wizard of Texas took the small, hard "Indian" peaches and experimented in artificial pollination in order to improve their characteristics and make them bigger and juicier. His neighbors laughed, but no one is laughing now. Every time you bite into a luscious Hill Country peach, you have Joseph Stubenrauch to thank.

    Tiny Stonewall, between Fredericksburg and Johnson City, is in the heart of peach country. Stonewallers celebrate their munificent crop with a peach of a festival each June. Here you can sample peach ice cream, peach freezes, and of course downhome peach pie and cobbler. In fact, there is hardly anything edible that can be made from a peach that hasn't been tried at one time or another.

Cookoffs!

**Third weekend in June
Chamber of Commerce
Stonewall 78671
(512) 644—9247**

Sulphur Springs
HOPKINS COUNTY STEW COOKOFF

At dawn, the first fires send smoke skyward and whiffs of burning wood begin to drift through the air. Before the sun is high, some fifty-odd fires will have cast-iron pots suspended over them. They await the ingredients that make up Hopkins County stew—potatoes, vegetables, meat (traditionally chicken), and the individual blends of herbs and spices that might make the pot this year's winner.

The stew that made Hopkins County famous had rather inauspicious beginnings. That is, it didn't impress anyone enough to warrant remembering the precise details. However, around the turn of the century, when Hopkins County had a population of about two hundred people, folks seemed to believe that the only way to cap off the school year was to commandeer a number of wash pots and throw a community stew social.

Following tradition, cookoff contestants concoct their entries in twenty- or thirty-gallon cast-iron pots over wood fires. These antiques are not in as short supply as you might think; as many as seventy-five have been counted simmering during this contest. The Hopkins County Chamber of Commerce will gladly help prospective contestants find one.

Cookoffs!

The stew cookoff climaxes a nine-day fall festival that features harvest displays, livestock exhibits, gospel-singing fests, carnival rides, and downhome contests like tobacco spitting, watermelon eating, and mule jumping.

The queen of the festival, known as the Cover Girl, is selected from local high school girls, who must have at least a B grade average and who must show themselves capable of the duties of a Hopkins County farm or ranch woman by demonstrating their ability to sew, cut up a chicken, decorate a parade float, back up a gooseneck trailer, milk a cow, rope a steer, saddle a horse, and bottle-feed a calf.

After the Cover Girl is announced, the judges bring the festival to a close by naming the best entry in the stew cookoff. Winners auction off batches for worthy causes and strollers can sample the entries by merely purchasing a bowl and spoon for a nominal fee.

Third Saturday in September
Hopkins County Civic Center
Ed Phelps
Hopkins County Chamber of Commerce
P.O. Box 347
Sulphur Springs 75482
(214) 885-6515

Taylor

INTERNATIONAL BARBECUE COOKOFF

The Blackland Prairies of Texas start on the right side of Interstate Highway 35, if you're heading north from Austin, in Central Texas. Oh, a narrow strip of them may continue on south and even west, but this black swath of earth doesn't widen and become prime farmland until about the time you get to Taylor, some twenty-five to thirty miles northeast.

It seems a quiet enough place, with big old Victorian houses in town, and cotton, wheat, and sorghum fields all around. In August, though, it livens up considerably for the annual barbecue cookoff. You can get good barbecue here anytime, at either Louie Mueller's or Rudy Mikeska's, so obviously the joy is in the game.

Cookoff contestants come from as far away as Maryland, the judges come from even more distant places (as well as Texas) for the privilege of participating in the event. In 1985 ninety-six teams heated up their smokers and slapped more than five hundred choice selections of beef, pork, seafood, poultry, mutton, goat, and wild game on the grills.

Cookoffs!

The judges select a favorite category and award points to the entrants. The points are toted up, and at the end the entrant with the most points is declared Master Cook. All the while, onlookers, kibitzers, and self-appointed tasters stroll by the pits, trying a sample here, a good chunk there. Even abstainers enjoy the entertainment put on by entrants in the showmanship category (look for the replica of a 1950s drive-in, complete with carhops on roller skates serving fountain Cokes and popcorn, while aspiring young mechanics gather around a group of museum-quality vehicles from that decade).

A few years ago, a Brooklyn dentist showed up at the barbecue cookoff. He was recognized as an outlander immediately because he was wearing a black T-shirt with a picture of the Brooklyn Bridge. He explained that he had discovered Texas barbecue while in the military service and had come back to relive the experience. Dr. Steve Markow has made three Taylor barbecues now and has served as a judge in the last two. Between cookoffs he has barbecue flown to him in Brooklyn. Sampling some prize-winning brisket, Dr. Markow said, "It's heaven. If this is what happens to you when you die, then come and get me."

Third Saturday in August
Murphy Park, Lake Drive, three blocks west of Texas Highway 95
Camille Berry
Taylor Chamber of Commerce
P.O. Box 231
Taylor 76574
(512) 352–2342

Terlingua

TERLINGUA COOKOFFS

When you get tired of looking at desert sunsets around the old mercury-mining ghost town of Terlingua, and when the movie crew packs up and leaves Lajitas, life can get a little routine. To break the monotony, Terlingua has cookoffs. In addition to the big chili cookoff, held the first weekend in November, this minuscule community in the Big Bend area has five more cookoffs every year.

Chronologically, the Cookie Chill-off in the middle of February comes first, though it is the oldest of the new events. Devised as a spoof on the chili cookoff, the chill-off involves no cooking whatsoever. Entries are limited to no-bake pies, cakes, and refrigerator cookies. Judges regularly include a number of journalists and perhaps a celebrity like John Henry Faulk, but the ground rules specify that the judging panel must always include a small child with a sweet tooth and Clay Henry, the famous beer-drinking goat from the Lajitas Trading Post. The idea for the Cookie Chill-off originated with Austin musician Steve Fromholz, who has an affinity for this part of West Texas, and it usually attracts a crowd of around three hundred. Daylong activities include a ten-kilometer fun run, continuous music, a bicycle race over the gravel roads and among the crumbling adobe ruins of Terlingua, and a tortilla toss (partial list of

Cookoffs!

rules: tortillas must be sailed; they may not be wadded and thrown; any contestant deliberately hitting a judge with his tortilla will be disqualified). A band comes from Austin for the evening dance.

The second annual W. Lee "Pappy" O'Daniel Biscuit Cookoff was held in Terlingua May 17. It takes its name from Texas Governor W. Lee O'Daniel (a flour salesman in private life), who held office from 1939 to 1941, during the period when Big Bend National Park was established.

On the Fourth of July, the Lajitas-on-the-Rio-Grande resort and the Lajitas Trading Post cosponsor a Bean Cookoff. The first-place winner in 1985 mistakenly cooked green beans, not realizing that "beans" meant pinto beans. Sponsors of the event refused to publicize the green-bean recipe out of acute embarrassment, so the recipe offered here is the second-place winner—with real pinto beans.

The Fajitas Fandango enlivens the desert the first weekend in September. Sponsored by the Woodward Ranch in Alpine, the 1985 event had lots of music and good food plus a strange new recipe for fajitas.

The winner of the Dutch Oven Cookoff, held on the second weekend in September, receives the Lajitas Cup and (in 1985, at least) a check for $1500 as well. The cookoff is sponsored by Lajitas-on-the-Rio-Grande, and other events include raft and canoe races in Colorado Canyon on the Rio Grande.

Saturdays in mid-February and mid-May, Fourth of July, and two Saturdays in September (see also Terlingua, World Championship Chili Cookoff)
Ghost town of Terlingua or Lajitas-on-the-Rio-Grande resort
Mimi Webb-Miller
Terlingua Foundation
P.O. Box 362
Terlingua 79852−0362
(915) 371−2234; or Bill Ivey, 424−3234

WORLD CHAMPIONSHIP CHILI COOKOFF

Chili is the official state dish of Texas—despite a lot of flak from a vociferous contingent that thinks it should be barbecue. The origin of chili is lost to recorded history, but it is known that in San Antonio around the turn of the century, a predecessor of today's chili was being sold on Military Plaza by women who were called chili queens. For a dime, plain folks and famous ones, like writer William Sydney Porter (better known as O. Henry) and orator William Jennings Bryan, could buy a bowl of one of the state's first fast foods.

It wasn't long before the Gebhardt company started selling chili powder and Lyman Davis began canning Wolf Brand chili. But chili was still just another stew until newspaperman Frank X. Tolbert of Dallas put it on the map. To publicize his book, *A Bowl of Red*, Tolbert staged a chili cookoff between Wick Fowler, a friend and fellow newspaper writer, and humorist H. Allen Smith. In 1967, the first World Championship Chili Cookoff was held in the desolate ghost town of Terlingua in the Big Bend area of Texas.

This cookoff, repeated annually, became famous, then infamous, and since then Texas has gone chili-cookoff crazy. As more and more cooks have decided that their special "bowl of blessedness" (as Will Rogers called his chili) was the world's best, cookoffs have proliferated. Contestants now have to accumulate points in regional cookoffs to earn the privilege of competing in the world championship, which has grown into a magnet for outrageous behavior and eccentric costumes of all types, attended by several thousand people annually.

First weekend in November
Ghost town of Terlingua
Mimi Webb-Miller
Terlingua Foundation
P.O. Box 362
Terlingua 79852-9362
(915) 371-2234; or Bill Ivey, 424-3234

Wichita Falls

TEXAS RANCH ROUNDUP COOKOFF

In the summer of 1980 an idea emerged from the offices of Falls Distributing Company and T. Brown Productions (both Anheuser-Busch distributors) that resulted ultimately in the creation of the Texas Ranch Roundup.

The thought behind the Ranch Roundup was, Why not return rodeo to its roots? Why not have real cowboys compete against each other in contests that resemble daily ranch work? And why not have these cowboys enter as members of teams from their ranches? Fourteen months later, twelve of the most historic Texas cattle ranches brought their teams to a hillside west of Wichita Falls and turned the clock back to the cattle-drive era. The Double U, the JA, the Pitchfork, the W. T. Waggoner, and the Spade ranches were among the competitors.

In order to enter the Ranch Roundup today, contestants must be full-time employees of their ranches and have been on the payroll at least six months. In addition to the arena events such as team roping, team penning, and branding, a talent contest is held, in which

Cookoffs!

ranch hands can compete in painting, photography, crafts, and music. A First Lady is named, judged on her ability to express her feelings on ranch life and demonstrate a working knowledge of her ranch.

In the cookoff portion of the Ranch Roundup, plain, honest chuck-wagon chow is prepared, such as meat, baked goods, and vegetables. Only natural fuel such as mesquite wood is permitted, and no "artificial" fuel (butane, charcoal briquettes) may be used. Granted, the food at this event may not have the gimmicky appeal of some other cookoff dishes; but to a tired cowboy, the idea of a smothered steak, a baked potato, and sourdough bread no doubt seems like heaven.

Mid-August, date to be announced
Sue Babb, Public Relations
North Texas Rehabilitation Center
516 Denver
Wichita Falls 76301
(817) 322–0771

Winnie

TEXAS RICE FESTIVAL

It may surprise you to learn that rice attracts some one hundred thousand people to this small town every October. Some of them come for the live entertainment, the livestock shows, and the art exhibits, but the rice industry takes center stage in the displays showing rice-farming machinery, in the educational exhibits, and of course in the various food booths.

Winnie's Texas Rice Festival has been going on for only sixteen years, but rice has been at home in Texas paddies since 1896. In that year, Jefferson County in East Texas had a rice mill and irrigation canals and produced the state's first rice crop. Despite droughts, hurricanes, and mosquitos, in only four years, rice cultivation had spread to twenty Gulf Coast counties.

The Texas Rice Festival packs a variety of activities into nine days each fall, with tournaments for softball, horseshoe pitching, and golf; a fun run; rice- and ice-cream-eating contests; fiddlers' and bluegrass-band competitions; parades; dances; and entertainment by popular local groups and nationally known celebrities. Spectator events vary, from the blessing of the rice fields to the coronation of a queen.

Cookoffs!

Today Texas rice goes around the world (three-fourths of the crop is exported) and even out of it (rice flew to the moon on *Apollo 14*). Some of the recipes developed for the Texas Rice Festival taste out of this world, too. Cooks in the rice-growing corner of the state have devised ways to get rice into every course from appetizers to dessert. It couldn't happen to a more deserving dish, the primary food for more than half the world's population.

First Saturday in October
Winnie-Stowell Chambers County Park
Susan Gaus or Monte Krebs
Texas Rice Festival
P.O. Box 147
Winnie 77665
(409) 296–4404

Chicken

TEXAS CHICKEN COOKING CONTEST

At one time the Texas Department of Agriculture and the Texas Poultry Federation jointly sponsored the Texas Chicken Cooking Contest. Cooks would send in their recipes, the recipes would be considered by a panel of judges, and the cooks who submitted the best five would be invited to Austin for a cookoff in the University of Texas Home Economics Department kitchens. The winner would get an expense-paid trip to the national cookoff, wherever that might be. In 1982, it was held in Dallas.

A couple of years ago, the National Broiler Council changed the procedure. Now recipes are sent directly to the national level, and the council enlists an independent panel of experts to select the state winners. These individuals still go to the national cookoff, which is held in odd years, alternating with the Pillsbury Bakeoff, held in even years.

Obviously, this is not a spectator sport, but, if you are interested in participating you may pick up an entry blank at your local grocery

Cookoffs!

store. They are also available from the sources listed below. The next contest is set for 1987.

Held odd years in different places
Bill Powers, Texas Poultry Federation, Austin
(512) 451–6816
Sponsored by the National Broiler Council
614 Madison Building
1155 Fifteenth Street NW
Washington, D.C. 20005
(202) 296–2622

ABOUT FAJITAS

First, if you aren't from Texas and you don't speak Spanish, you'll want to know that the correct pronunciation is "fah-*hee*-tas." The word refers to the cut of beef—skirt steak—that these morsels come from. In the last decade fajitas have become the most prevalent Tex-Mex food around. Most items of the genre, such as guacamole and tacos, are served exclusively in Mexican restaurants, but fajitas can appear on almost any menu that serves American or Southwest cuisine.

It is astonishing how superb this inexpensive cut of meat is after being properly marinated and grilled. Some purists insist that only a mesquite fire will do, but in fact you can cook fajitas perfectly well in a skillet on top of a conventional stove.

The proper way to serve fajitas, which are traditionally cut into strips about half-an-inch wide by about four inches long, is rolled in a hot flour tortilla. They are further enhanced by the addition of *pico de gallo* (freshly chopped onion, tomato, chile peppers, and cilantro), sour cream, grated cheese, and guacamole (mashed-avocado salad).

Cookoffs!

Terrific fajitas can be found at Fast Eddie's down in Port Isabel. Eddie's hokey converted filling station is filled with cookoff trophies for everything from barbecue to chili to, of course, fajitas. Even if you don't order anything to eat, the stories, jokes, and pointers on prize-winning cooking will keep you in stitches.

Note:
All the fajita recipes in this book were winners in specific fajita cookoffs across the state. Because fajita cookoffs abound, and the scheduling of these events varies from year to year, not all the recipes included have a corresponding festival entry.

Soups, Salads, and Appetizers

Black-eyed Pea Wheels
Black-eyed Pea Jamboree, Athens

1 15-ounce can black-eyed peas, drained
½ stick butter or margarine
1 dash garlic powder
2 dashes cayenne pepper
¼ teaspoon Lawry's seasoned salt
6 ounces cream cheese
8 slices (ounces) imported ham
8 green onions

Heat peas in melted butter. Add garlic, cayenne pepper, and seasoned salt. Simmer for 15 minutes. Cool and blend together with softened cream cheese in food processor until mixture is creamy and well combined. Spread mixture onto each slice of ham, then roll one green onion lengthwise in each piece of ham. Chill and cut into ½-inch wheels. Serves 8.

Billy Archibald, Mexia

Cookoffs!

Pea-ta Bread Filled with Zuc-pea-ni Salad
Black-eyed Pea Jamboree, Athens

PEA-TA BREAD:
5 or 6 cups unsifted flour
2 teaspoons salt
1 tablespoon sugar
1 package dry yeast
2 cups warm water (105°–115°)
1 cup black-eyed peas, cooked and drained

In a large bowl mix thoroughly 2 cups flour, salt, sugar, and undissolved dry yeast. Gradually add warm water to dry ingredients and beat 2 minutes at medium speed, scraping bowl occasionally. Add ¾ cup flour. Beat at high speed 2 minutes. Stir in enough additional flour to make a soft dough. Turn out onto lightly floured board. Knead in 1 cup peas until smooth and elastic, about 8 to 10 minutes. Place in a greased bowl, turning the dough to grease it. Cover, let rise in a warm place free from drafts for about 1 hour, until doubled in bulk.

Punch dough down, turn out onto a lightly floured board, cover, and let rest 30 minutes. Divide dough into 6 equal parts and shape each into a ball. On a lightly floured board, roll each ball into an 8-inch circle. Place on a lightly floured baking sheet. Slide the baking sheet onto the bottom rack of a very hot oven (450°) or into a preheated iron skillet placed on the lowest rack of a very hot oven. Bake about 5 minutes or until done (tops will not be brown). Brown tops in broiler about 3 inches from heat for about 1 minute. Watch closely to prevent burning. Serves 12.

ZUC-PEA-NI SALAD

2 cups black-eyed peas, cooked, drained, and chilled
1 cup raw zucchini squash, shredded
2 cups fresh spinach, shredded
2 cups cooked chicken, cubed
1 egg, boiled and finely chopped
½ cup celery, finely chopped
½ cup bell pepper, finely chopped
Onion, grated, to taste
Sprinkle of Tony Chachere's Creole seasoning
½ cup mayonnaise
½ cup sour cream
Cubed tomato, shredded cheese, and alfalfa sprouts (for garnish)

Mix together all ingredients (except garnishes) and place in pockets of halved Pea-ta Bread rounds. Top with tomatoes, cheese, and alfalfa sprouts. Serves 12.

Joanna Goldman, Marshall.

Creole Fresh Corn Soup
Texas Rice Festival, Winnie

2 tablespoons cooking oil
2 tablespoons flour
2 pounds fresh shrimp, peeled and deveined
1 onion, chopped
2 cloves garlic, chopped
1 tablespoon sugar
1½ teaspoons salt
1¼ teaspoons pepper
4 cups uncooked corn, freshly cut from cob
½ cup green onion tops, chopped
3 ounces tomato paste
2 quarts water

In a 4-quart pot, cook oil and flour to make a brown roux. Add shrimp and cook, stirring often, until shrimp are golden brown, about 10 minutes. Add onions and garlic and cook another 3 to 5 minutes. Add seasonings and continue to cook stirring over a low fire. Add corn and cook for about 15 minutes, stirring. Add green onion tops, tomato paste, and water. Simmer slowly for 30 minutes longer, adding more water if too thick. Serve over rice. Serves 8.

Nell Key, Fannett

Jalapeño and Rice Salad
Jalapeño Festival, Laredo

2 cups rice, cooked
3 tablespoons celery, chopped
3 tablespoons olives stuffed with pimientos, chopped
1 tablespoon green onions, chopped
3 tablespoons jalapeños, chopped
1 jar artichokes, drained and chopped (reserve liquid)
1 cup mayonnaise
1 teaspoon sugar
Parsley, chopped (for garnish)

Mix first 6 ingredients together. Mix mayonnaise, liquid from artichokes, and sugar together and blend into rice mixture. Chill. Sprinkle top with parsley. Serves 4.

Miriam Gutierrez, Laredo

Chicken Hors d'Oeuvres Olé
Feather Fest, Nixon

3 fryers
⅓ cup onion, coarsely chopped
⅓ cup bell pepper, coarsely chopped
⅓ cup celery, coarsely chopped
½ cup lemon juice, with pulp
Dash garlic powder
Dash ground cumin
6 7-ounce cans Herdez Mexican green hot sauce
½ cup green onions, finely chopped
½ cup bell pepper, finely chopped
½ clove fresh garlic, finely chopped
3 tablespoons cooking oil
3 tablespoons flour
2 teaspoons salt
1 teaspoon pepper
2 teaspoons fresh cumin, finely ground
1 teaspoon Ac'cent (MSG)
1½ cups sour cream
Round tortilla chips, approx. 2 inches in diameter
    (3 dozen per fryer)
2 8-ounce cartons sour cream, for garnish
Chopped parsley, cilantro, green onions, or
    jalapeños (for garnish)

Pressure-cook whole chicken in small amount of water with the ⅓ cup each of onion, bell pepper, and celery, and lemon. Season lightly with dash of garlic powder and cumin. When chicken is cooked, cool, skin, debone, and cut it up with kitchen shears.

Soups, Salads, and Appetizers

While chicken is cooking, heat green hot sauce in medium pot with dash of garlic powder. Keep warm. Chop green onions, bell pepper, and fresh garlic for chicken hors d'oeuvres topping.

Put 3 tablespoons cooking oil into a large, heavy pot. Sauté green onions, bell pepper, and garlic. Add flour seasoned with next 4 ingredients and brown lightly. Fold in 1½ cups sour cream and stir until smooth. Add cut-up chicken and blend well. Heat and keep warm. If too dry, add a little chicken broth. Warm chips and spread each with chicken topping, finishing with green hot sauce. Garnish with sour cream and choice of chopped parsley, cilantro, green onions, or jalapeños. The recipe may also be served on chalupa or taco shells. Each chicken yields 3 dozen hors d'oeuvres.

Franco Villa Company, Nixon

Alligator Logs
Texas Rice Festival, Winnie

2 pounds alligator, deboned
½ cup celery, chopped
½ cup onion, chopped
¼ cup bell pepper, chopped
2 teaspoons creole crab boil
1 cup cooked rice
¼ teaspoon garlic, minced
Salt and pepper to taste
1 cup Italian-style bread crumbs
½ cup chicken broth
Additional Italian-style bread crumbs

Pressure-cook alligator meat until tender, about 1 hour. Sauté celery, onion, and bell pepper. Flake alligator meat in food processor. Combine alligator and other ingredients, adding broth last. Shape into 2- to 3-inch logs. Roll in bread crumbs and deep-fry at 365° until golden brown. Makes about 3 dozen.

Dewayne Leger, Winnie

Tortilla Soup
Feather Fest, Nixon

SOUP
3 whole chickens
3 onions, chopped
1 rib celery, chopped
2 cans hot Ro-tel tomatoes
1 can regular Ro-tel tomatoes
6 cloves garlic
1 cup cilantro, chopped
Salt and pepper to taste
2 tablespoons comino

GARNISH
6 avocados, sliced
32 ounces sour cream
30 corn tortillas, cut in bite-sized pieces and fried

Boil whole chickens in salted water with onions and celery for 1 hour. Debone chicken and return meat to the pot. Add remaining ingredients and simmer 30 minutes. Garnish with sour cream, avocado slices, and tortilla pieces before serving. Serves 16.

Ben Talamantez, Nancy Talamantez, Megg Laijas, Chuck Laijas, Nixon

Jalapeño Jelly
Jalapeño Festival, Laredo

⅓ cup jalapeños, seeded and chopped (see directions)
1 cup bell pepper, chopped
6½ cups sugar
1½ cups apple cider vinegar
6 ounces pectin
2 to 3 drops green food coloring

Remove seeds and white veins from jalapeños before chopping for a mild jelly; leave in for a hot, spicy jelly. Cook jalapeño and bell peppers, sugar, and vinegar for 10 minutes. Remove from fire and strain (you may wish to leave some flecks of pepper if you removed the seeds). Add pectin and coloring and stir well. Place in jars and seal. Makes 6 half pints.

Vegetables and Pasta

Fettuccine Southwest
Feather Fest, Nixon

½ cup sour cream
1 cup whipping cream
2 teaspoons fresh lime juice
½ pound fettuccine, fresh or dried
Salt
6 ounces cooked chicken, sliced
20 young, tender spinach leaves, sliced into strips
6 mild green chiles, fresh or canned, rinsed and sliced into strips
16 medium fresh mushrooms, sliced
¼ cup Parmesan cheese

Make crème fraîche by combining sour cream, cream, and lime juice. Let stand at room temperature at least 2 hours to thicken. Refrigerate.

Gently boil pasta in salted water until al dente (30 seconds to 1 minute for fresh pasta). Drain, but leave a small amount of water on pasta. Put in a large skillet. Add chicken and vegetables, toss, and heat slowly. (The water left on the pasta should keep it from scorching.) Add about 1 cup crème fraîche. Warm thoroughly and serve immediately with Parmesan cheese sprinkled on top. Makes about 4 cups cooked fettuccine.

Chuck Bloom, Nixon

Campfire Potatoes
Texas Ranch Roundup Cookoff, Wichita Falls

6 baking potatoes
1 stick butter melted
6 strips bacon

Scrub each potato, cut in half, make slits, and fill with butter. Put the halves of each potato back together and wrap in a piece of bacon. Secure with a toothpick. Wrap in aluminum foil and place in hot coals in a fire pit. Bake 25 to 30 minutes. Serves 6.

Billy George Drennan,
Pitchfork Land and Cattle Company, Guthrie

Just Plain Ol' Black-eyed Peas
Black-eyed Pea Jamboree, Athens

4 cups fresh black-eyed peas
Salt and pepper, to taste
1/4 teaspoon paprika
1 pound salt pork, cubed
1 pound pork sausage, coarsely crumbled and fried
1 tablespoon granulated beef base
1/4 tablespoon cayenne pepper
1/2 cup bacon grease
1 cup pork broth

Cover black-eyed peas with water, add seasonings and salt pork, and bring to a boil. Reduce heat and cook slowly about 2 hours. Add remaining ingredients and simmer another 30 minutes or until peas are tender. Serves 8.

Charlotte Parks, Ben Wheeler, Texas

Cajun-Style Pinto Beans
Bean Cookoff, Terlingua

3 pounds dried pinto beans
½ cup rum
1 8-ounce bottle liquid crab boil
½ teaspoon nutmeg
1 teaspoon oregano
1 teaspoon cumin
1 teaspoon dill weed
1 teaspoon cayenne pepper
2 tablespoons salt

Wash beans and remove any bad ones. Cover with water and soak overnight. Mix all ingredients. Cook until beans are tender, adding water as needed. Serves 15.

Mike Kutzer, Lajitas

Bread

Onion Italian Bread
Onion Festival, Noonday

2 cups water
1 tablespoon butter
5 to 6 cups flour
1 tablespoon salt
1 tablespoon sugar
2 packages dry yeast
1 cup onion, chopped
1 clove garlic, minced
¼ cup butter or margarine
1 egg white
1 tablespoon cold water
1 tablespoon sesame seeds

Heat 2 cups water and 1 tablespoon butter to 120°–130°. In a large bowl, combine 2 cups flour, salt, sugar, and yeast. Using electric mixer, beat water and butter in gradually to form a soft batter. Then beat 3 minutes at medium speed to develop gluten. Stir in enough more flour to make a soft, workable dough. Turn out onto a floured surface and knead 5 to 10 minutes, adding flour as needed. Place dough in a greased bowl, turn, and cover. Let rise until doubled in volume, about 1½ hours. Punch dough down and let rise another 30 to 45 minutes.

While dough is rising, sauté onion and garlic in melted ¼ cup butter or margarine until onions are browned and tender. Set aside and let cool to room temperature.

After second rising of the dough, turn it out onto a floured surface and divide in half. Roll first half to ½-inch thickness. Spread half of onion mixture over dough, leaving a 1-inch margin. Roll into a tight, oblong loaf. Tuck ends under and place the loaf seam down on a greased cookie sheet sprinkled with cornmeal. Repeat with remaining dough. Cover each loaf with a towel and let rise 30 to 45 minutes.

(continued on next page)

Cookoffs!

Preheat oven to 425°. Slash tops of loaves diagonally 3 times. Whisk egg white with 1 tablespoon cold water, brush over loaves, and sprinkle with sesame seeds. Bake 30 to 45 minutes until golden brown. Makes 2 loaves.

Diane Smotherman, Tyler

Panocha Bread
Panocha Bread Cookoff, Edinburg

2½ pounds flour, approximately
1 teaspoon salt
2 teaspoons baking powder
5 teaspoons lard
2 cups water

Mix first 3 ingredients, cut in lard, and add enough water to make a soft dough. Grease a large cast-iron skillet (16 inches across by 5 inches deep), and heat it and its lid in mesquite coals for about 5 minutes. Roll the dough out until about 1 inch thick, place in skillet, cover, and return to fire, placing hot coals on lid. Cook about 10 minutes, longer if necessary. Makes 1 loaf.

Julian Betancourt, Edinburg

Cookoffs!

White Bread
Gillespie County Fair, Fredericksburg

½ cup warm water (105–115°)
2 packages dry yeast
1 teaspoon sugar
2 cups warm water (105–115°)
5 tablespoons sugar
1½ teaspoons salt
3 tablespoons shortening
7 cups white flour

In a small bowl, mix ½ cup warm water, yeast, and 1 teaspoon sugar. Stir and set aside for 5 minutes. In a large bowl, mix 2 cups warm water, 5 tablespoons sugar, salt, shortening, and yeast mixture. Add flour gradually. Knead dough for 10 minutes. Put dough in greased bowl, cover, and let rise until double in volume. Turn out on floured board and knead a couple of times. Divide dough in half. Place each half in a greased loaf pan. Let rise until almost double in volume. Bake at 350° for 35 minutes. Makes 2 loaves.

Ursula Worrell, Fredericksburg

Whole Wheat Bread
Gillespie County Fair, Fredericksburg

2 packages dry yeast
2 cups warm water (105°–115°)
1 teaspoon sugar
2 cups warm milk (105°–115°)
⅓ cup shortening
½ cup brown sugar
2 tablespoons salt
3 cups whole wheat flour
6¾ to 7 cups white flour

Stir yeast into warm water with sugar. Let dissolve for 5 minutes. Add warm milk, shortening, brown sugar, and salt to water-and-yeast mixture. Add whole wheat and white flour and mix. Knead 10 minutes. Return to greased bowl, cover, and let rise in a warm place until double in volume (about 1½ hours). Divide dough in half, and place each half in a greased loaf pan. Let rise again until almost double in volume. Bake at 350° for 40 minutes. Makes 2 loaves.

Ursula Worrell, Fredericksburg

Rye Bread
Gillespie County Fair, Fredericksburg

2 packages dry yeast
3½ cups warm water (105°–115°)
1 teaspoon sugar
⅓ cup shortening
½ cup molasses
2 tablespoons salt
2 tablespoons caraway seeds
3 cups rye flour
6 to 7 cups white flour

Stir yeast into warm water together with 1 teaspoon sugar. Let dissolve for 5 minutes. Add shortening, molasses, and salt. Stir well. Add caraway seeds and rye and white flour. Knead for 10 minutes. Return dough to greased bowl, cover, and let rise until double in volume (about 1½ hours). Divide dough in half and place each half in a greased loaf pan. Let rise until again almost double in volume. Bake at 375° for 40 minutes. Makes 2 loaves.

Ursula Worrell, Fredericksburg

Pumpernickel
Gillespie County Fair, Fredericksburg

4 cups white flour
2 cups rye flour
½ cup cornmeal
1 tablespoon salt
1 package dry yeast
2 cups water
¼ cup molasses
1 ounce unsweetened chocolate
1 tablespoon shortening
1 cup mashed potatoes
1 teaspoon caraway seeds

Combine white and rye flour. Remove 1½ cups mixed flours and blend with cornmeal, salt, and yeast in a large bowl. Heat water, molasses, chocolate, and shortening in a saucepan until very warm (120°–130°), stirring occasionally. Gradually add the liquid to the flour-and-yeast mixture, combining thoroughly. Add mashed potatoes, 1 more cup of the mixed flours, and caraway seeds. Mix well and add remaining flour. Knead for 10 minutes. Return to greased bowl, cover, put in warm place, and let rise until double in volume (about 1½ hours). Divide dough in half. Place each half in a greased loaf pan. Let rise until almost double in volume. Bake at 350° for 45 minutes. Makes 2 loaves.

Ursula Worrell, Fredericksburg

Bacon Cornettes
Potlatch, Carthage

12 slices bacon
1 cup self-rising flour*
1 cup self-rising cornmeal*
¼ cup sugar
2 eggs, well beaten
1 cup milk

Fry bacon until crisp, drain, and crumble, reserving ¼ cup drippings. Combine flour, cornmeal, and sugar. Add eggs, milk, and reserved bacon drippings. Stir until moistened and add crumbled bacon. Spoon batter into greased muffin tins and bake at 425° for 20 to 25 minutes. Makes 1 dozen.
  *If regular flour and cornmeal are used, add 3 teaspoons baking powder and ½ teaspoon salt to dry ingredients.

Amy Clabaugh, Carthage

Seafood Hushpuppies
Southern Hushpuppy Olympics, Lufkin

½ cup flour
½ cup cornmeal
1 heaping teaspoon sugar
½ teaspoon garlic powder
½ teaspoon cayenne pepper
½ teaspoon coriander
½ teaspoon creole seasoning or chili powder
1 heaping tablespoon parsley, chopped
1 heaping tablespoon green onion, chopped
1 heaping tablespoon pimiento, chopped
1 heaping tablespoon boiled shrimp, chopped
1 heaping tablespoon lump crabmeat, chopped
1 heaping tablespoon fresh crawfish tails, chopped
1 egg, slightly beaten
½ cup milk, approximately

Stir dry ingredients together and then add remaining ingredients, using just enough milk to moisten the batter. Place in a pastry bag fitted with a large star-shaped tip and swirl batter into 365° cooking oil in a deep-fat fryer. Turn hushpuppies once and cook until golden brown. Remove, drain, and salt if desired. Makes 1 dozen large hushpuppies.

Parker Folse, Dallas

Jalapeño Hushpuppies
Southern Hushpuppy Olympics, Lufkin

2 cups white cornbread mix
2 tablespoons flour
3 eggs, slightly beaten
1 bunch green onions (about 6 stalks), chopped
1 white onion, chopped
½ cup milk, approximately
Salt and pepper to taste
1 tablespoon jalapeños, chopped

Combine cornbread mix, flour, and eggs. Add onions and enough milk to make the mixture tacky. Add salt, pepper, and jalapeños. Shape, using a small round ice cream scoop, and fry in hot oil until golden brown. Makes 2 dozen.

Boyd McGaugh, Meridian, Mississippi

Spicy Hushpuppies
Southern Hushpuppy Olympics, Lufkin

1 cup flour
1 cup yellow cornmeal
1 teaspoon baking powder
½ teaspoon salt
½ cup trical flour
¼ cup milk
2 eggs, slightly beaten
1 teaspoon hot pepper sauce
1 teaspoon mild cherry pepper, minced
1 teaspoon garlic, minced
1 teaspoon green onion, minced
1 teaspoon pimientos, chopped
3 tablespoons cream-style corn

Mix dry ingredients, add liquids, then seasonings and corn, and mix well. Heat cooking oil in a deep-fat fryer to 365° and drop batter in by teaspoonfuls. Cook until brown, turning once. Drain. Makes 2 dozen.

O. O. "Shotgun" Wright, Dallas

Original Longneck Biscuits
W. Lee "Pappy" O'Daniel Biscuit Cookoff, Terlingua

2 cups flour
1 tablespoon baking powder
1 teaspoon salt
½ cup shortening
¾ cup milk
Butter, melted

Sift dry ingredients into a large bowl. Cut in shortening until mixture attains a uniform, crumblike texture. Stir in milk with a fork until dough is fairly free from sides of bowl. Knead briefly with fingertips and roll out 1 inch to 1½ inches thick on a floured surface. Cut biscuits as desired. Place on greased baking sheet, brush tops with melted butter, and bake about 10 minutes in a 450° oven. (The biscuits may be baked in a Dutch oven over hot coals; line the bottom of the pot with aluminum foil to prevent them from burning.) Makes 15.

Reed Allen, Houston

Cowboy Crêpes
Texas Ranch Roundup Cookoff, Wichita Falls

5 cups sourdough starter
3 cups flour
6 eggs
1 teaspoon salt
4 tablespoons cooking oil
3 cups milk
2 cups apricots, peeled, sliced, and sweetened, or
   2 cups blueberries, sweetened
½ cup sour cream
Powdered sugar

Combine sourdough, flour, eggs, salt, oil, and milk, adjusting flour and milk to make a thin pancake batter. Cook crepes on a griddle. Cool and top each with 1 tablespoon apricots or blueberries and ½ teaspoon sour cream. Roll and sprinkle with powdered sugar. Makes 2 to 3 dozen.

Glenda Shobe, Double U Hereford Ranch, Levelland

Chili

Fast Eddie's Chili
Rio Grande Valley Livestock Show, San Benito

4 medium yellow onions, finely chopped
3⅓ pounds beef brisket, 80% lean, coarsely ground
4 tablespoons paprika
3 1½-ounce envelopes Chili-Quik
1 15-ounce can tomato sauce

Boil onions until tender. Drain, reserving water. Simmer meat in onion water until done, about ten minutes. Drain liquid, sprinkle meat with paprika, and add onions, Chili Quik, and tomato sauce. Simmer 4 hours. Serves 12.

FAST EDDIE'S, Port Isabel

Cowgirl Chili
National Cowgirl Hall of Fame Chili Cookoff, Hereford

½ cup olive oil
3 pounds beef, coarsely ground
3 cloves garlic, chopped
1 large onion, chopped
3 large fresh green (unripe) tomatoes
6 to 8 fresh New Mexico green chiles
Salt and pepper, to taste

In a heavy pot, fry meat in olive oil until lightly brown on all sides. Remove from pot. Sauté garlic and onion in the oil until translucent. Add green tomatoes and chiles to onions, and sauté. Return meat to pot, add water to cover, and simmer, covered, for about 2 hours. Stir occasionally to prevent sticking. Add water if necessary.

This green chili is great alone or served on flour tortillas with plenty of picante sauce. Serves 12.

Richard Forrest, Hereford

"Old Snort" Chili
Winner of Three Chili Cookoffs in 1985

3 pounds beef, coarsely ground
2 ounces chili powder (such as Gebhardt's) or
   ground red chili peppers
1 clove garlic
1 large onion, chopped
¼ teaspoon cayenne pepper
¼ teaspoon paprika
¼ teaspoon curry powder
¼ teaspoon marjoram
1 teaspoon dry mustard
1 15-ounce can tomato juice
1 15-ounce can water
Salt, to taste
1 tablespoon masa flour
1 can jalapeños (optional)

Cook meat until lightly done, pouring liquid off peridiocally and reserving. Then fry meat in frying pan until light brown. Return reserved liquid to frying pan. Add remaining ingredients except salt and *masa* flour. Cook slowly 1 hour, adding salt to taste, starting with 1 teaspoon. Make a paste of *masa* flour and water and mix with the meat. Simmer another 20 to 30 minutes; correct seasoning. (Add more chili powder if recipe is too mild, or some liquid from a can of jalapeños). Serves 12.

Janie and Bill Mohler, San Angelo

North Texas Red Chili
Chilympiad, San Marcos

4 pounds beef, cubed or coarsely ground
2 tablespoons shortening
1 10¾-ounce can beef broth
2 large onions, chopped
1½ cups Gebhardt's chili powder
2 tablespoons cumin
1 teaspoon oregano
3 teaspoons garlic salt
1 16-ounce can tomato sauce
4 canned jalapeños (stems removed)
1 teaspoon cayenne pepper
Salt, to taste

Brown meat in shortening. Add broth and enough water to cover the meat. Add onions and cook 30 minutes. Add remaining ingredients (pierce the jalapeños 2 or 3 times with a knife, cook until tender, strain, and stir pulp into the chili). Cook 3 hours over low heat, adding water if needed and salt to taste. Serves 16.

Tom Tyler, Mesquite

Wes Ritchey's Hat-Pin Chili
World Championship Chili Cookoff, Terlingua

2 pounds beef, cubed
3 tablespoons dried minced onion
2 teaspoons cumin
½ teaspoon garlic powder
½ teaspoon salt
½ teaspoon Ac'cent (MSG)—optional
¼ teaspoon oregano
⅛ teaspoon white pepper
⅛ teaspoon cayenne pepper
1 teaspoon green jalapeño sauce
1 8-ounce can tomato sauce
2 beef bouillon cubes
6 tablespoons salt-free chili powder
2 teaspoons cumin
½ teaspoon Ac'cent (MSG)—optional
¼ teaspoon garlic powder
⅛ teaspoon white pepper
⅛ teaspoon cayenne pepper
1 pinch basil

Brown beef in a large pot for about 30 minutes or until it turns gray. Add next 11 ingredients (through bouillon cubes) and water to cover. Simmer 1¾ hours, stirring occasionally and adding water as needed. Then add remaining ingredients except basil. Simmer 45 minutes, stirring occasionally and adding more water as needed. Ten minutes before serving, add basil. Adjust salt, cayenne, cumin, and chili powder, if necessary.

If desired, reduce cayenne pepper to a pinch, and substitute a large, fresh jalapeño pepper. Slit skin and float whole pepper in chili. Remove after 45 minutes and squeeze in the juice, but not pulp or seeds. Serves 8.

Wes Ritchey, Garland

Cookoffs!

Jim Ivey's Community Chili
World Championship Chili Cookoff, Terlingua

3 pounds chuck roast, cubed
1 8-ounce can tomato sauce
1 medium onion, chopped
3 fresh jalapeños, stems removed
4 tablespoons chili powder
3 tablespoons cumin
1 teaspoon garlic powder
1 teaspoon paprika
½ teaspoon oregano
1 teaspoon Ac'cent (MSG)—optional
1 teaspoon pepper
½ teaspoon cayenne pepper

Put meat, tomato sauce, and onion in a large pot with water to cover. Wash and prick jalapeños and drop them in, whole. Add 1 tablespoon each of chili powder and cumin. Bring to a boil, cover, and reduce heat. Cook until tender (2 to 2½ hours), adding more water as needed.

Remove jalapeños, put them through a strainer, and add juice to the chili. (Discard pulp.) Put the remaining spices in a cup or bowl, cover, and shake to mix. Add about half the mixture to the pot about 30 minutes before chili is done. Add rest of spice mixture about 15 minutes before chili is done. Serves 12.

Jim Ivey, Irvin

Meats and Main Courses

Szechwan Rabbit
Rabbit Fest, Copperas Cove

¼ cup soy sauce
1 tablespoon cornstarch
2 rabbits, boned and diced
½ cup cooking oil
1 medium green pepper, coarsely chopped
1 medium onion, coarsely chopped
1 8-ounce can sliced water chestnuts, drained
2 Fresh jalapeños or serranos, seeded and chopped
2 cloves garlic, minced
1 teaspoon fresh ginger root, chopped
2 tablespoons soy sauce
2 tablespoons cornstarch
1 tablespoon sugar
1 teaspoon cayenne pepper
¼ cup plus 1 tablespoon water
1 tablespoon vinegar
1 tablespoon Chablis or other dry white wine
1 tablespoon Szechwan chile sauce

Combine ¼ cup soy sauce and 1 tablespoon cornstarch in a large bowl; stir in rabbit and let stand 30 minutes. Pour oil around top of a preheated wok, coating sides. Maintain at medium heat (325°) for 2 minutes. Add undrained rabbit pieces and stir-fry about 2 to 3 minutes, until meat is lightly browned. Remove rabbit and set aside, reserving pan drippings in wok. Add next 6 ingredients and stir-fry for 2 minutes. Combine last 8 ingredients and add to vegetables in wok. Add rabbit and cook until liquid is thickened, stirring constantly. Serve over rice. Serves 6 to 8.

John Hansel, Pflugerville

Barbecued Rabbit
Rabbit Fest, Copperas Cove

RABBIT
1 3-pound rabbit
1 8-ounce bottle Green Goddess salad dressing

Cover rabbit with salad dressing, wrap in foil, and cook 3 hours over a barbecue pit. Uncover, baste with barbecue sauce, and cook uncovered 1 more hour. Serve 4.

BARBECUE SAUCE
1 16-ounce bottle Smokehouse barbecue sauce
4 ounces beer
¼ cup soy sauce
¼ cup Worcestershire sauce
½ cup brown sugar
2 tablespoons dry mustard

Mix all ingredients, bring to a boil, and simmer until thoroughly blended. Use to baste rabbit. Serves 3 to 4.

Station KOOV, Copperas Cove

Cookoffs!

Big Boys' Best Chicken
International Barbecue Cookoff, Taylor

5 tablespoons brown sugar
1½ tablespoons Lawry's seasoned salt
1 tablespoon lemon pepper seasoning
½ teaspoon garlic powder
10 chicken wings or thighs
Additional Lawry's seasoned salt
Additional lemon pepper seasoning

Mix brown sugar with seasoned salt, lemon pepper seasoning, and garlic powder. Roll chicken in it twice. Sprinkle with additional seasoned salt and lemon pepper seasoning. Smoke for 2 to 2½ hours. Serves 5 to 10.

"Chicken Martha" Smith, Carrollton

Lime Roasted Chicken
Texas Chicken Cooking Contest

1 whole chicken
¼ cup fresh lime juice
¼ cup cooking oil
½ teaspoon salt
⅛ teaspoon pepper
1 tablespoon parsley, chopped
1 tablespoon capers
2 carrots, cooked and cut in strips lengthwise
3 potatoes, boiled, peeled, and cut in wedges
2 leeks, both green and white parts, cut lengthwise
½ pound mushrooms, halved
1 lime, sliced (for garnish)

Place chicken in roasting pan. Pour over it and inside its cavity a mixture of lime juice, cooking oil, salt, pepper, parsley, and capers. Marinate about 1 hour, turning often. Bake at 400° for 20 minutes; turn and baste; bake 20 minutes more. Turn and baste again, and then add carrots, potatoes, leeks, and mushrooms. Bake 20 minutes more or until fork can be inserted into chicken with ease. Garnish with lime slices. Carve chicken and serve with vegetables, spooning juices over all. Serves 4.

Hollis F. Talburt, Houston

Cookoffs!

Chicken El Greco
Texas Chicken Cooking Contest

4 whole chicken breasts, deboned and skinned
½ teaspoon salt
½ teaspoon pepper
¼ teaspoon garlic salt
¼ cup flour
2 tablespoons olive oil
1 cup sour cream
1 tablespoon lemon juice
¼ teaspoon oregano
1 large tomato, cut in 4 thick slices
4 teaspoons margarine, divided in fourths
½ cup ripe olives, sliced
1 tablespoon parsley, chopped

Skin and debone chicken breasts. Rub salt, pepper, and garlic salt onto the chicken and dredge in flour. In a large, ovenproof frying pan, heat olive oil to medium temperature. Cook chicken, turning, about 10 minutes, or until brown on all sides. Mix sour cream, lemon juice, and oregano and spoon over chicken. Cover and bake in preheated 350° oven for about 30 minutes, or until a fork can be inserted in chicken with ease. Remove chicken from oven, place 1 tomato slice on each piece and 1 teaspoon margarine on each tomato. Sprinkle with olives and parsley and return to oven about 10 minutes or until tomatoes are tender. Serves 4.

Barbara Chesser, Waco

Chicken Boursin
Texas Chicken Cooking Contest

2 whole chicken breasts, halved, deboned, and skinned
½ teaspoon salt
¼ teaspoon pepper
⅓ cup flour
1 5-ounce package herbed Boursin cheese
4 slices Prosciutto ham
3 tablespoons butter
1 tablespoon cooking oil
½ pound mushrooms, sliced
4 scallions, chopped
2 tablespoons brandy
1 cup chicken broth
½ cup white vermouth
¼ cup parsley, chopped
½ teaspoon salt
¼ teaspoon pepper

On hard surface with meat mallet or similar utensil, pound meat to ¼-inch thickness. Sprinkle ½ teaspoon salt and ¼ teaspoon pepper on the chicken and dredge in the flour, one piece at a time. Spread about 2 tablespoons of the cheese on one side of each piece of chicken. Place 1 slice of ham on top of cheese. Roll up each piece of chicken and fasten with wooden picks. In a frying pan, place butter and oil and heat to medium temperature. Add rolled chicken and cook, turning, about 5 minutes or until slightly brown. Add mushrooms and scallions and sauté for 5 minutes. Add brandy and ignite. When flame goes out, add chicken broth, vermouth, and parsley; stir to mix. Cover and simmer about 30 minutes, or until fork can be inserted in chicken with ease. Stir in remaining ½ teaspoon salt and ¼ teaspoon pepper. Serves 4.

Billie Venable, Dallas

Texas Hot Chicken
Texas Chicken Cooking Contest

¼ cup cooking oil
2 large tomatoes, sliced
2 large onions, sliced
8 chicken thighs
½ cup evaporated milk
4 cloves garlic, minced
1½ tablespoons brown sugar
1½ teaspoons lemon juice
2 teaspoons red pepper flakes
1½ teaspoons salt
¼ teaspoon mace
2 bay leaves

Put oil in a large frying pan and heat to medium temperature. Add tomatoes and onion and cook about 5 minutes or until wilted. Add chicken, stirring several times. Add remaining ingredients and bring to a boil. Cover and simmer, stirring frequently, for 30 minutes. Remove cover and cook 10 more minutes over high heat until most of liquid has evaporated and a fork can be inserted into chicken with ease. Remove bay leaves before serving. Serves 4.

Loanne Chiu, Arlington

"A Touch of the Tropics" Chicken Salad
Texas Rice Festival, Winnie

3 cups chicken, cooked and cubed
3 cups cooked rice, cooled
1 cup celery, sliced or chopped
¼ cup bell pepper, chopped
2 20-ounce cans pineapple tidbits
2 8-ounce cans mandarin oranges
1½ tablespoons lemon juice
2 teaspoons salt
¼ teaspoon pepper
½ cup mayonnaise
½ cup sour cream
½ teaspoon curry powder
½ cup almonds, sliced

Mix chicken, rice, celery, and bell pepper and chill. Drain pineapple tidbits and oranges. In a separate bowl, blend lemon juice, salt, pepper, mayonnaise, sour cream, and curry powder. Just before serving, mix all ingredients together. Serves 6.

Tia Pair, Winnie

Cookoffs!

O.R.* Special for Barbecued Chicken
Feather Fest, Nixon

CHICKEN SOP (Marinade)
3 cups white wine
1 stick margarine, melted
1 dash Tabasco
1 teaspoon garlic, minced
1 tablespoon Worcestershire sauce
1 dash salt
1 dash pepper
1 dash fajita seasoning
Juice of 1 lemon
1 onion, cut in quarters

Mix ingredients and slowly inject into chicken. If you are not a doctor and don't have a hypodermic handy, you could try marinating (or sopping) the chicken. This amount should handle 3 chickens.

BARBECUE SAUCE:
6 cups tomato sauce
2 tablespoons ketchup
1 teaspoon sugar
3 fresh green and 3 dried red chiles
¼ cup butter, melted
¼ cup vinegar
Salt and pepper, to taste
1 dash garlic powder

Mix ingredients and slowly simmer 45 minutes. Brush over chicken during last 15 minutes of cooking. Makes 6 cups.

*Operating Room

David Vincent, Nixon.

Chicken Surprise
Feather Fest, Nixon

1 whole chicken
1 onion, diced
1 bell pepper, chopped
3 cups celery, chopped
¾ cup margarine
¾ cup Coffee Rich
1 cup Velveeta cheese
1 can condensed cream of mushroom soup
1 can condensed cream of celery soup
½ package onion soup mix
1 16-ounce can tomatoes
Garlic salt and pepper, to taste
½ teaspoon chicken bouillon
1 15-ounce can asparagus
1 4-ounce can mushrooms
8 hash-brown potato baskets, frozen

Boil whole chicken in salted water for 1 hour. Debone. Sauté onion, bell pepper, and celery in margarine. Add Coffee-Rich, Velveeta, soups, tomatoes, garlic salt, pepper, bouillon, and chicken meat. Simmer 5 minutes. Add asparagus and mushrooms.

Fry potato baskets, fill with chicken mixture, and serve hot. (Hash-brown potato patties may be substituted for the baskets.) Serves 8.

Ken Borchardt and Beverly Talley, Nixon

Chicken Stew
Hopkins County Stew Cookoff, Sulphur Springs

24 to 25 pounds whole chickens
12 pounds potatoes, cubed
10 pounds onions, chopped
8 46-ounce cans tomatoes or 4 large cans tomato juice
Salt to taste
Black and cayenne pepper to taste
2 cans chili peppers or to taste
2 pounds butter
9 16-ounce cans cream-style corn
3 16-ounce cans whole-kernel corn

Boil chicken in salted water until tender. Reserve broth. Debone chicken, cut into small pieces, and set aside. Put potatoes, onions, broth from chicken and enough water to cover in a large pan. Simmer 1 hour. Then add tomatoes, chicken meat, seasonings, and chile peppers. Simmer about 2 more hours or until aroma indicates ingredients are well blended. Add butter and corn 30 minutes before serving. (The recipe's creators say the secret is cooking the stew over a wood fire and stirring frequently.) Makes 12 to 15 gallons.

Nell Sparkman and Donna Reed, Sulphur Springs

Hopkins County Chicken Stew
Hopkins County Stew Cookoff, Sulphur Springs

2 4-pound whole chickens
22 ounces tomato juice
2 teaspoons chili powder
4 cups chicken stock (from cooking the chickens)
2 cups water
1 28-ounce can tomatoes
1½ pounds onions, chopped
1 teaspoon granulated chicken base
5 pounds potatoes, peeled and cut in chunks
1 28-ounce can corn
1 teaspoon salt, or to taste

Boil chickens in salted water until done. Debone. Marinate the chicken meat overnight in tomato juice and chili powder. Bring stock and water to a boil and add tomatoes, onions, and chicken base. Bring to a boil again and add chicken meat and potatoes. Simmer 20 minutes until potatoes are tender. Add corn and salt and heat thoroughly. Serves 8 to 10.

Polly Walters and Glenda Mitchell, Sulphur Springs

Sweet-and-Sour Dove
Fiesta de la Paloma and Dove Cookoff, Coleman

10 to 12 uncooked dove breasts, cut in bite-size pieces
1 cup red wine
3 tablespoons oil or butter
3 tablespoons soy sauce
1 clove fresh garlic, grated fine
⅓ cup brown sugar
1 medium bell pepper, chopped
1 15¼-ounce can pineapple chunks and syrup
½ cup vinegar
Salt to taste

Marinate dove breast pieces in red wine at least 2 hours, longer if possible. Drain. Sauté 5 minutes in oil or butter in a heavy pan or iron skillet. Mix remaining ingredients together and add. Simmer 45 minutes. Serve over steamed rice with garlic toast as an accompaniment. Serves 2.

Rosa Baker, Coleman

Glazed Duckling with Apricot Rice
Texas Rice Festival, Winnie

DUCKLING
1 5-pound duckling
½ teaspoon salt
1 12-ounce jar plum preserves
¼ cup light corn syrup
¼ cup orange juice
1 teaspoon orange peel, grated
¼ teaspoon ginger
¼ cup toasted slivered almonds

Salt duck, place on rack in shallow pan, and roast at 325° for 2 hours. Meanwhile, in a saucepan combine plum preserves, corn syrup, orange juice and peel, and ginger. Bring to a boil and cook 1 minute. Spoon glaze over duck several times during last 30 minutes of baking. Sprinkle almonds and remaining glaze over duck. Serve with apricot rice. Serves 3 to 4.

APRICOT RICE
1 1-pound can apricot halves
1 tablespoon butter or margarine
1 6-ounce package long-grain and wild rice, with
   seasonings
½ teaspoon orange peel, grated

Drain apricot halves, reserving syrup. Add enough water to syrup to make 2½ cups liquid. In a large saucepan, combine liquid and butter and bring to a boil. Stir in rice and contents of seasoning packets. Cover and simmer for 25 minutes or until liquid is absorbed. Remove from heat and stir in apricot halves and orange peel. Arrange around glazed duck.

Kriste Whatley, Baytown

Cookoffs!

Texas Barbecued Shrimp
International Barbecue Cookoff, Taylor

2 packages Italian salad dressing mix
2 medium onions, cut in 1-inch squares
3 bell peppers, cut in 1-inch squares
1½ pounds thick-sliced bacon
5 pounds jumbo shrimp, peeled and deveined
1 jar barbecue sauce
1 clove garlic, minced
Pepper, coarsely ground, to taste
1 can beer
¼ cup Worcestershire sauce
1 stick butter (do not use margarine)

Prepare Italian salad dressing according to package instructions and set aside.

Put onions, peppers, bacon, and shrimp on skewers, wrapping bacon around shrimp. When each skewer is full, insert another skewer from the opposite end to prevent shrimp from rotating and cooking unevenly. To the barbecue sauce add minced garlic, black pepper, beer, Worcestershire sauce, and butter. Heat and stir until thoroughly mixed.

Place skewers over red-hot coals. Baste shrimp generously with Italian dressing, turning frequently. About halfway through the cooking process, begin basting with barbecue sauce. It will burn, so alternate with Italian dressing. Barbecue sauce may be thinned with beer if too thick. Cook until shrimp turn light-pink. Serves 20.

First Taylor National Bank Cooking Team
David Schmidt, head cook, Taylor

Barbecued Goat
Goat Cookoff, Brady

1 cabrito (very young goat), cut in pieces
2 large onions
8 ounces lemon juice
12 ounces vegetable oil
8 ounces bottled Italian dressing
1 bottle barbecue sauce, with smoke
2 or 3 cans beer

Place pieces of goat in a large pan. Chop onions in a blender and mix with lemon juice, vegetable oil, and 4 ounces of the dressing. Simmer in a saucepan until onions are cooked. Pour over meat and wrap in foil. Refrigerate and let tenderize 5 hours. Smoke goat in a smoker 3 to 4 hours, basting with a mixture of barbecue sauce, the remainder of the Italian dressing, and beer (sauce will be thin). Brown in smoker and serve. Serves 6.

Richard Jackson, Ronnie Horton, and Ezra Horton, Llano

Barbecued Cabrito
Goat Cookoff, Brady

1 cabrito (very young goat), cut in half
Salt and pepper, to taste
1 pint lemon juice
1 pint lime juice
10 ounces Worcestershire sauce
16 ounces liquid Italian dressing
1 pint corn oil
12 cans beer

Salt and pepper both halves of goat. Mix liquids, pour over goat, refrigerate, and marinate at least 12 hours. Drain and cook very slowly 3 to 4 hours over mesquite coals until meat is tender. Serve with flour tortillas. Serves 6.

Cedar Hut Gang, Sinton

Sauce for Barbecued Lamb
Lamblast, San Angelo

1 cup butter
1 cup brown sugar
1 cup Worcestershire sauce
1 onion, chopped
1 4-ounce can mushrooms
6 jalapeños, chopped
1 can beer (optional)
1 lemon, halved

Melt butter, add next 5 ingredients, and simmer a few minutes. Add can of beer if you wish. Rub lamb with the lemon. Barbecue lamb, basting with sauce during last half hour of cooking. Makes 4 cups.

Ern Whitley, Mertzon

Les Inman's Barbecue Sauce
Wild Game Cookoff, Llano

2 medium onions, sliced
2 sticks margarine
1 6-ounce jar mustard
1 15-ounce bottle cooking oil
1 16-ounce bottle white vinegar
4 lemons, thinly sliced
2 teaspoons Worcestershire sauce
1¼ teaspoons Louisiana red hot sauce
1 tablespoon Lawry's seasoned salt
1 can Lone Star beer
2 tablespoons A.1. Sauce
2 tablespoons brown sugar (optional)

In a large, heavy saucepan, sauté onions in margarine. Add remaining ingredients except A.1. Sauce and sugar. Simmer until well blended, 15 to 30 minutes. Add A.1. Sauce and simmer another 30 minutes. If desired, add brown sugar. Use to baste any barbecued meat. Makes 7 cups.

Les Inman, Llano

Meats and Main Courses

Deep-Fried Wild Hog
La Salle County Wild Hog Cookoff, Cotulla

5 pounds wild hog ribs, separated (pork ribs will do in a pinch)
2 cans evaporated milk
2 cups self-rising flour
1 teaspoon Morton's Nature seasoning
1 teaspoon salt
½ teaspoon pepper

Marinate ribs in mixture of half evaporated milk and half cold water for at least 4 hours, in refrigerator. Blend flour and seasonings. Drain ribs, dredge in flour mixture, then in water and milk mixture, and back in flour. Fry in hot oil at least 3 inches deep until done. Serves 4.

Jonaid "Hog Wild" Tiller, Cotulla

Cookoffs!

Grand-Prize Hamburger
Uncle Fletch Davis Memorial World Hamburger Cookoff, Athens

6 ounces top ground sirloin (20% fat)
Garlic salt, salt, and pepper to taste
Kikkoman teriyaki sauce
Hamburger bun
Mayonnaise
Mustard
Leaf lettuce
Tomato, sliced
Red onion, sliced
Avocado, sliced
Monterey Jack cheese, grated

Season meat with garlic salt, salt, and pepper, and cook over charcoal to desired doneness, glazing with teriyaki sauce. Grill onion slices and warm buns. To prepare buns, mix mayonnaise and mustard, spread on both buns, and place ingredients on bottom bun in the following order: lettuce, tomato, meat, onion, avocado, cheese, and top bun. Makes 1 hamburger.

David Knouse and Dick Woodward,
Tolbert's Texas Chili Parlor, Dallas

Colossal Chicken-fried Steak
Chicken-fried Steak World Championship, Big Spring

1 pound round steak
4 ounces canned sliced jalapeños
½ teaspoon garlic salt
¼ teaspoon salt
¼ teaspoon black pepper
1 tablespoon chili powder
1½ tablespoons paprika
1 dash ginger
2 cups Wondra flour
2 eggs
2 cups milk
5 strips bacon

Cut steak into 4 pieces and pound until thin. Marinate in jalapeño juice (with jalapeños) at least 30 minutes. To the flour add garlic salt, salt, pepper, chili powder, paprika, and ginger. Beat eggs with a fork and add milk. Fry bacon, remove from pan, and add cooking oil as needed for frying the steaks. Dip marinated meat in milk mixture and then in flour. Fry at moderate temperature (350° in electric skillet). Garnish with bacon. Serves 4.

Dave Wrinkle, Big Spring

Ranch-Style Smothered Steak
Texas Ranch Roundup Cookoff, Wichita Falls

1 to 2 pounds round steak
1 cup flour
½ teaspoon salt
¼ teaspoon pepper
6 tablespoons cooking oil
1 can condensed cream of mushroom soup
1 can water
1 cup milk, warmed

Cut steak in four pieces and dredge in flour mixed with salt and pepper. Fry in hot oil until brown. Remove meat. In the frying pan, mix soup, water, milk, and steak drippings. Put steaks in a baking pan and pour soup mixture over them. Bake at 350° for 1 hour. (Can also be cooked in a covered heavy pan over coals.) Serves 4.

Kay Petit, Cowan & Son Circle Bar Ranch, Seymour

Rum Fajitas
Fajitas Fandango, Terlingua

2 pounds skirt steak
1 cup Bacardi light rum
1 8-ounce jar liquid crab boil

Marinate and refrigerate meat overnight in rum and crab boil. Cook over mesquite coals. Slice into 4-inch strips. Serves 6.

Mike Kutzer, Lajitas

Cookoffs!

Outlaw Fajitas
Pioneer Days Fajita Cookoff, Fort Worth

5 pounds skirt steak
Fajita seasoning (Jiminez is excellent)
20 limes
1 quart beer
1 jar Pickapeppa sauce
1 jar Woody's barbeque sauce
1 tablespoon Lawry's seasoned salt, or to taste
1 tablespoon pepper, or to taste
6 onions, cut in wedges

Sprinkle meat with fajita seasoning mix and place in a large, deep pan. Squeeze lime juice over the meat, and put the lime peels in the pan. Cover with beer and add Pickapeppa and barbecue sauce, seasoning salt, and pepper. Marinate 24 hours in the refrigerator.

Build a hot charcoal fire over a grill (soak mesquite chips in water to create smoke). Put the whole skirt steaks and lime peels on the grill. Turn the grill frequently, basting the meat with marinade. Add onion wedges, and cover. Cook 10 to 15 minutes.

When done, cut meat in 4-inch-long strips, place in a small pan, add marinade, and reheat. Serve rolled in flour tortillas with assorted garnishes. Serves 20.

Jim Lane, Fort Worth

Meats and Main Courses

Fast Eddie's Fajitas
Fajita Cookoff, Austin

3 pounds skirt steak
Lemon-pepper seasoning
Garlic powder
8 ounces soy sauce
2 cups pineapple juice
1 small can crushed pineapple
2 ounces Figaro liquid smoke
6 ounces Worcestershire sauce
8 ounces canned tomato sauce
1 quart beer
2 medium onions, sliced

Tenderize steak with a meat mallet. Sprinkle liberally with lemon-pepper, garlic powder, and soy sauce. Marinate seasoned meat 24 hours in a mixture of the next 6 ingredients. (Pour carefully so as not to wash off seasonings.)

Slice meat into strips about 4 inches long and place in a noncorrosive pan. Cover with sliced onions and cook in pan over a mesquite fire (do not cook over direct flame). Serves 8 to 12.

FAST EDDIE'S, Port Isabel

Tamale and Corn Fiesta
Potlatch, Carthage

1 tablespoon butter
½ large onion, chopped
1 17-ounce can cream-style corn
1 can Wolf Brand tamales, cut in bite-size pieces (reserve liquid)
8 ounces sour cream
1 cup Fritos, crushed
10 ounces cheddar cheese, grated
2 tablespoons jalapeños, sliced (for garnish)
Additional Fritos, crushed (for garnish)

Sauté onion in a mixture of butter and liquid from tamales. Mix corn, tamales, and onion in a deep-dish pie pan. Bake at 350° for about 45 minutes. Add sour cream, 1 cup of the Fritos, and grated cheese. Return to oven and bake just until the cheese melts. Garnish with additional Fritos and jalapeños. Serves 4.

Kay Majors, Carthage

Green Chili Enchiladas
Dutch Oven Cookoff, Terlingua

12 corn tortillas
2 tablespoons cooking oil
2 cans condensed cream of chicken soup
2 small cans green chiles, or 8 to 10 roasted fresh green chiles (not jalapeños)
¼ teaspoon garlic powder
½ cup evaporated milk
1 pound cheddar cheese, grated
Black olives, sliced (for garnish)
Additional cheddar cheese (for garnish)

Fry tortillas for a few seconds in hot oil and set aside. Heat soup, chiles, garlic powder, and milk, until bubbly. Dip tortillas one at a time in the mixture. Sprinkle grated cheese on each tortilla and stack one on top of another in the Dutch oven. Cover with remaining sauce, black olives, and more grated cheese. Cook over hot coals (and place some on top of lid) until thoroughly heated and cheese is melted. Serves 4.

Darlene Estes, Lajitas

Cookoffs!

Crusty Oatmeal Quiche
Oatmeal Festival, Bertram and Oatmeal

1⅓ cups quick-cooking oats
⅓ cup whole wheat flour
2 tablespoons grated Parmesan cheese
6 tablespoons margarine, melted
2 tablespoons water
1 dash salt
3 eggs
½ cup light cream
¼ teaspoon salt
1 dash pepper
½ cup ham, cooked and diced
⅔ cup broccoli, cooked and chopped
2 tablespoons onion, finely chopped
¾ cup Swiss cheese, grated

Combine oats, flour, Parmesan cheese, margarine, water, and salt. Press into a 9-inch pie pan and bake at 325° for 5 minutes. Cool. Combine eggs and cream and mix well. Stir in remaining ingredients. Pour into pie shell and bake at 325° for 30 to 35 minutes or until an inserted knife comes out clean. Makes 1 quiche.

Sharon Goodwin, Bertram

Seafood Gumbo
International Gumbo Cookoff, Orange

1 cup vegetable oil
1 cup flour
1 large white onion, minced
½ bell pepper, minced
1 large rib celery, minced
1 pound lump crabmeat
1 pound fresh shrimp, deveined and peeled
2 packages dried shrimp, soaked overnight in
  1 cup water
1 pound crawfish tails, cleaned
1½ quarts water
2 cloves garlic, minced
½ teaspoon salt, or to taste
¼ teaspoon cayenne pepper, or to taste
1 teaspoon Ac'cent (MSG)
1½ cups green onions, chopped
¼ cup parsley, chopped
2 teaspoons gumbo filé powder (optional)

Make a roux by stirring oil and flour in a large iron pot over low heat until light brown. Reserve a half cup to add later. Sauté onion, bell pepper, and celery in roux. Add all seafood and stir-fry for 2 or 3 minutes. Add water, garlic, salt, cayenne pepper, and Ac'cent. Bring to a hard boil and then reduce heat and simmer for 20 to 25 minutes. Add green onions and parsley and simmer 10 more minutes. Add reserved roux gradually if needed to thicken. Serve over hot steamed rice, seasoning with filé if desired. Serves 12.

Juanita Young, Orange

Sausage and Seafood Combination Gumbo
International Gumbo Cookoff, Orange

½ cup oil
1 cup flour
1 cup celery, chopped
1 cup onions, chopped
½ cup green onions, chopped
2 pounds crawfish tails, peeled
2 pounds shrimp, peeled and deveined
½ pound crabmeat
2 pounds smoked sausage, sliced
½ teaspoon cayenne pepper
1 teaspoon garlic powder
1 teaspoon black pepper
1 teaspoon salt, or to taste

In a large Dutch oven, make a roux of oil and flour, stirring until chocolate brown in color. Remove from heat. Add vegetables and hot water until pot is half full. Return to heat, add seafood, sausage, and seasonings. Simmer 30 minutes. Serve over steamed rice. Serves 16.

R. J. Wells and Crew, Orange

Guinea Gumbo
International Gumbo Cookoff, Orange

3 whole guinea hens
2 Cornish hens
2 cloves garlic, chopped
2 teaspoons oregano
Salt and pepper, to taste
Cayenne pepper, to taste
Creole seasoning, to taste
White pepper, to taste
5 to 6 ribs celery, chopped
4 onions, chopped
3 bunches green onions, sliced
1 small bell pepper, minced
1 cup flour
1 cup oil

Cut guinea and Cornish hens into small pieces and season with next 6 ingredients listed. Put in a covered container and refrigerate overnight.

Boil water in a large pot, add chicken, and cook until almost done. Add vegetables and cook until meat is tender.

Make a dark brown roux by cooking the oil and flour, add to pot, and stir until roux dissolves. Continue simmering slowly to reduce liquid. Correct seasoning. Serves 8.

Debra Denmon and Jess Kid, Orange

Desserts and Pastries

Cherry Layer Cake
Gillespie County Fair, Fredericksburg

CAKE
2½ cups sifted cake flour
1½ cups sugar
3½ teaspoons baking powder
1 teaspoon salt
½ cup shortening
¾ cup milk
¼ cup maraschino cherry juice
1 teaspoon vanilla
2 teaspoons almond extract
4 egg whites, unbeaten
18 maraschino cherries, well drained and finely chopped
½ cup pecans, chopped

Sift cake flour, sugar, baking powder, and salt into a mixing bowl. Cut in shortening. Combine milk and cherry juice. Add ¾ cup of this liquid and the vanilla and almond extract. Beat 2 minutes at medium speed, scraping bowl several times. Add remaining liquid and the egg whites. Beat 2 minutes. Fold in cherries and pecans. Bake in two 9-inch greased cake pans at 375° for 20 to 25 minutes. (May need up to 10 minutes additional baking time.) Makes one 2-layer cake.

(continued on next page)

Cookoffs!

FROSTING
½ cup shortening
6 cups sifted powdered sugar
¼ teaspoon salt
2 teaspoons vanilla
⅓ cup maraschino cherry juice
1 cup pecans, chopped
5 or more whole maraschino cherries

Beat shortening, half of powdered sugar, salt, and vanilla until light and fluffy. Add cherry juice and remainder of powdered sugar alternately. Continue to beat until light and fluffy again. Add chopped pecans. Spread on cherry layer cake. Decorate top with cherries.

Dana Herber, Fredericksburg

Rum Cream Pie
Messina Hof Winefest, Bryan

6 egg yolks
1 cup sugar
1 envelope unflavored gelatin
½ cup cold water
1 pint whipping cream
½ cup light rum
1 graham cracker crust, baked
Chocolate, grated (for garnish)

Beat egg yolks and sugar until light. In a small saucepan, dissolve gelatin in cold water. Bring to a boil, stirring constantly. Pour gelatin into the egg mixture continuing to stir constantly. Let cool until almost thick. Whip cream until stiff and add it and the rum. Bake crust. Chill filling 45 minutes and then pour into the cooked crust. Sprinkle chocolate on top. Chill until firm. Makes 1 pie.

Joan McDonald, Bryan

Cookoffs!

Yam Pie
Yamboree, Gilmer

2 cups cooked sweet potatoes
2 cups sugar
½ cup cream or evaporated milk
½ cup butter, softened
1 egg
1½ teaspoons vanilla
1 unbaked 9" pie shell

Mash potatoes. Mixed with other ingredients and beat until light (about 5 minutes with electric mixer). Pour in unbaked pie crust. Bake at 350° about 50 minutes. Makes 1 pie.

Carolyn Bassham, Gilmer

Frozen Strawberry Rice Pie
Texas Rice Festival, Winnie

CRUST
¾ cup flour
¾ stick margarine
½ cup pecans, chopped
¼ cup powdered sugar

Cut margarine into flour until mixture is size of small peas. Add pecans and powdered sugar and mix well. Press into a 9- or 10-inch pie pan. Bake at 320° for 20 minutes. Cool before filling. Makes 1 pie.

FILLING
½ pint whipping cream
½ pound cream cheese
½ cup sugar
1½ cups frozen strawberries
1½ envelopes unflavored gelatin
4 tablespoons strawberry juice
1 cup cooked rice
1 baked pie shell (recipe above)

Whip cream and set aside. Soften cream cheese and blend with sugar in a mixing bowl until fluffy. Defrost and drain strawberries, reserving juice. Add strawberries to cream cheese mixture. Heat reserved juice from strawberries and dissolve gelatin in it. Combine gelatin and cream cheese mixtures, add rice, and mix well. Fold in whipped cream. Turn into pie shell and chill. Makes 1 pie.

Mrs. Ernest LaFleur, Winnie

Cookoffs!

Rancho El Milagro Lime Pie
Cookie Chill-Off, Terlingua

CRUST
1 box chocolate wafers
2 tablespoons sugar
¾ stick butter, softened

Mix ingredients together and press into a greased 9-inch pie pan.

FILLING
1 can sweetened condensed milk
Juice of 6 limes, or to taste
2 drops green food coloring
Lime slices (for garnish)
Fresh mint (for garnish)

Blend ingredients and pour into crust. Refrigerate at least 3 hours. Top with lime slices and sprigs of mint. Makes 1 pie.

Mimi Webb-Miller, San Carlos, Chihuahua, Mexico

Susie Maude's Coconut Cream Pie
Messina Hof Winefest, Bryan

1¾ cups milk
¾ cup sugar
½ teaspoon salt
1½ tablespoons flour
2 tablespoons cornstarch
1 whole egg, beaten
2 eggs, separated
2 tablespoons butter, softened
½ teaspoon vanilla
½ cup flaked coconut
1 9-inch pie shell, baked
1 cup whipping cream, whipped
¼ cup flaked coconut (for garnish)

Scald half the milk and add ½ cup sugar and salt. Bring to a boil and keep at a simmer. Mix flour, cornstarch, beaten whole egg, and egg yolks with the remaining unscalded milk. Beat until smooth. Add a little of the hot milk mixture and blend. Gradually combine both mixtures and cook over low heat until thick, stirring constantly. When mixture bubbles, remove and add the butter and vanilla. Beat with electric mixer until smooth.

Place egg whites in another bowl and beat until frothy. Slowly add remaining ¼ cup sugar and beat until stiff. Fold the custard lightly into the beaten egg whites; do not blend thoroughly. Sprinkle ½ cup coconut into the mixture and pour into a baked pie shell. Spread with whipped cream, sprinkle on remaining coconut, and chill. Makes 1 pie.

Dianne Woods, Iola

Grandma Krenek's Pecan Pie
Messina Hof Winefest, Bryan

3 tablespoons butter
⅔ cup light brown sugar
1 dash salt
3 eggs
¾ cup light corn syrup
½ cup milk
¾ teaspoon vanilla
1 cup pecans
1 unbaked 9" pie shell
1 cup whipping cream, whipped (optional)

Cream butter and slowly beat in brown sugar and salt. Add eggs one at a time and beat briskly. Blend in other ingredients. Pour into pastry shell. Bake 10 minutes at 450°, then reduce heat to 350° and bake until custard sets, about 30 minutes. Serve plain or with whipped cream. Makes 1 pie.

Carolyn Krenek, Bryan

Peach Cobbler
Peach Jamboree, Stonewall

8 cups fresh peaches, sliced
⅓ cup flour
2 cups sugar
1 teaspoon cinnamon
½ cup butter or margarine, melted
1 teaspoon almond extract
1 recipe pastry dough (using 2 cups flour)

Dredge peaches in flour, add next 4 ingredients, and mix well. Roll out half of dough to 8 by 16 inches, cut in half, and place halves in the bottom of two 8-by-8-inch square pans. Bake at 475° for 8 minutes. Remove from oven and spoon half of peach mixture into each pan. Roll out remaining pastry, cut into strips, and arrange in a latticework over peaches. Bake at 350° for 1 hour. Makes 2 pies.

DeAnn Weinheimer, Stonewall

Country Peach Pie
Peach Jamboree, Stonewall

1 cup sugar
1½ tablespoons cornstarch
1½ tablespoons tapioca
½ teaspoon cinnamon
¼ cup water
1 teaspoon butter
3 cups fresh peaches, sliced
1 unbaked 9-inch pie shell
Pastry for latticework (optional)
Crumb topping (optional)

Mix first 6 ingredients together in a saucepan and cook over low heat until the mixture thickens and barely comes to a boil. Add to the peaches and cool. Pour peaches into the pie shell and top with a latticework crust or a crumb topping. Sprinkle with sugar and cinnamon and bake at 325° for 1 hour or until filling bubbles and pastry is golden brown. Makes 1 pie.

Mildred Jenschke, Albert

Grandma's Oatmeal Crisps
Oatmeal Festival, Bertram and Oatmeal

1 cup shortening, melted
1 cup brown sugar
1 cup white sugar
2 eggs, well beaten
1 teaspoon vanilla
1 cup shredded coconut
1 cup pecans
1 cup flour, sifted
1 teaspoon salt
1 teaspoon baking soda
4 cups quick-cooking oats

Combine shortening and brown and white sugar. Add eggs, vanilla, coconut, and pecans. Mix remaining dry ingredients, including oats, and add to first mixture. Shape into 1-inch balls and place on a greased cookie sheet. Bake at 350° for 10 to 12 minutes. Makes about 5 dozen.

Sharon Goodwin, Bertram

Cookoffs!

Pinwheels
Winter Garden Pecan Bake Show, Hondo

1 cup flour
¾ teaspoon salt
¼ teaspoon baking powder
½ cup brown sugar
¼ cup butter, softened
1 egg yolk
½ teaspoon vanilla
1 6-ounce bag chocolate chips
1 tablespoon butter
1 cup pecans, chopped
⅓ cup sweetened condensed milk
1 teaspoon vanilla
¼ teaspoon salt

Sift first three ingredients. Beat brown sugar and ¼ cup butter until fluffy and blend in egg yolk and ½ teaspoon vanilla. Stir into flour mixture. Roll into a 9-by-12-inch rectangle.

Melt together chocolate and 1 tablespoon butter. Stir in pecans, milk, vanilla, and ¼ teaspoon salt. Spread over cookie dough and roll tightly. Wrap in foil and chill until firm. Cut into ¼-inch slices and bake at 350° for 10 minutes. Makes 4 dozen.

Cathy Moore, Knippa

Corn Flake Macaroons
Gillespie County Fair, Fredericksburg

2 egg whites
1 cup sugar, sifted
1 cup coconut
1½ cups corn flakes, lightly crushed
1 teaspoon vanilla

Beat egg whites until stiff. Add sugar very gradually and continue beating until sugar is well blended with whites. Fold in other ingredients. Drop by teaspoons onto a well-greased cookie sheet. Bake in a slow oven, 300°–325°, for 20 to 25 minutes. (Cookies will be crisper in dry weather.) Makes about 3 dozen.

Jerome Jenschke, Fredericksburg

Skillet Cookies
Gillespie County Fair, Fredericksburg

1 stick margarine
1 cup sugar
1 egg, slightly beaten
1 tablespoon corn syrup
1 cup dates, chopped
1 cup pecans, chopped
2 cups Rice Krispies
2 cups coconut

Mix first 6 ingredients in a heavy skillet. Cook 10 minutes over low heat, stirring often. Cool slightly and add Rice Krispies. Shape into walnut-size balls, flatten, and roll in coconut until coated. Makes 4 dozen.

Jerome Jenschke, Fredericksburg

Texas Strawberry Riesling Ice Cream
Texas Ice Cream Crank-off, Austin

2½ cups Texas Riesling wine (Fall Creek or equivalent)
4 eggs
½ cup sugar
½ cup honey
1¼ cups strawberries, finely sliced
⅓ cup pecans, finely chopped
1 cup whipping cream
1 cup light cream
Strawberries, sliced (for garnish)

Place wine, eggs, and sugar in top of a double boiler and beat thoroughly with a whisk. Place over boiling water. Stir mixture constantly until it is thick enough to coat a spoon (takes time). Do not overheat mixture or allow it to boil. When proper thickness is reached, chill mixture in refrigerator.

In a separate bowl, mix together the honey, strawberries, and pecans and chill. Place custard mixture in ice-cream-freezer container and add whipping cream and light cream. Process until it begins to thicken then add the strawberry mixture. Continue freezing to desired firmness. Serve with sliced strawberries. Makes 1 gallon.

Carolyn Croom, Austin

Cookoffs!

Strawberry Cheesecake Ice Cream
Texas Ice-Cream Crank-off, Austin

2 cups sugar
¼ teaspoon salt
2 cups milk
4 eggs
3 cups strawberries, quartered and divided in two portions
⅓ cup brown sugar
8 ounces cream cheese
¾ cup half-and-half
1 tablespoon lemon juice
1 tablespoon vanilla
¾ cup pecans, finely chopped
Milk

Combine sugar, salt, and milk in container of a food processor or blender. Blend until sugar is dissolved. Add eggs and continue blending until well mixed. Place in a saucepan and cook over medium heat, stirring constantly, until mixture begins to thicken (about 10 minutes). Refrigerate 4 hours or overnight.

Add brown sugar to the quartered strawberries, stir well to dissolve sugar, and set aside. When ready to freeze, combine half of the custard and all the cream cheese in container of a food processor or blender. Process until smooth. Pour into chilled 1-gallon freezer container.

Combine the remaining custard, half the strawberries, the half-and-half, lemon juice, and vanilla. Process until smooth and pour into the freezer container. Add remaining strawberries and pecans. Add milk to fill ⅔ full, if needed. Freeze according to instructions. Allow to ripen at least an hour to develop flavor. Makes 1 gallon.

Barbara Gilbert, Austin

Pistachio Fudge Nut Ice Cream
Ice Cream Crank-off at Ashton Villa, Galveston

2 eggs
1 cup sugar
1/8 teaspoon salt
1/2 box instant pistachio pudding mix
2 cups milk
2 cups light cream
1 tablespoon almond extract
3 drops green food coloring
1/2 cup unsalted pistachios, chopped
1 6-ounce jar fudge topping

Beat eggs until frothy. Add remaining ingredients except nuts and fudge topping. Beat until sugar and pudding dissolve. Pour into ice-cream-freezer container and process until thick. When nearly ready to serve, fold in nuts and fudge topping and freeze to desired firmness. Makes 1/2 gallon.

Ida Diamond, Galveston

Cookoffs!

"Ashton Villa Vanilla" Ice Cream
Ice Cream Crank-off at Ashton Villa, Galveston

4 eggs, well beaten
2 cups sugar
⅛ teaspoon salt
4 cups whipping cream
2 cups milk
2 tablespoons vanilla
2 cups milk

Beat eggs until fluffy; then stir in sugar and salt until dissolved. Add whipping cream, 2 cups milk, and vanilla flavoring. Pour mixture in ice-cream-freezer container and add remaining 2 cups milk, leaving 4 inches empty at the top of the can. When fully processed, pack additional ice and salt around freezer container and freeze until firm. Makes 1 gallon.

Marge Scheffield, Galveston

Red-White-and-Blueberry Ice Cream
Ice Cream Crank-off at Ashton Villa, Galveston

2 eggs
1 cup sugar
⅛ teaspoon salt
½ box instant vanilla pudding
2 cups milk
2 cups half-and-half
1½ teaspoons vanilla
1 cup sweetened blueberries
1 cup sweetened strawberries
1 cup sweetened raspberries

Beat eggs until frothy. Add next 6 ingredients and beat until sugar and vanilla pudding mix dissolve. Pour into ice-cream-freezer container and process. When fully processed, fold in berries and freeze until firm. Makes ½ gallon.

Ida and Lou Diamond, Galveston

Cookoffs!

"Texas Mud" Ice Cream
Ice Cream Crank-off at Ashton Villa, Galveston

2 eggs
1 cup sugar
⅛ teaspoon salt
½ box instant chocolate pudding
2 cups milk
2 cups half-and-half
1½ teaspoons vanilla
1 teaspoon chocolate extract
¼ teaspoon cinnamon
1 cup marshmallow cream
1 cup small marshmallow pieces
1½ cups chocolate brownies, crumbled
½ cup pecans, finely chopped

Beat eggs until frothy. Add next 8 ingredients. Beat until sugar and pudding mix dissolve. Pour into ice-cream-freezer container and process until thick. Fold in last 4 ingredients and freeze to desired firmness. Makes ½ gallon.

Ida and Lou Diamond, Galveston

Onion Praline Ice Cream
Onion Festival, Noonday

PRALINE
2 cups Noonday sweet onions, chopped*
¼ cup butter
1 cup sugar
¼ cup water
1 cup pecans, coarsely chopped

Sauté onions in butter until translucent. Drain. Caramelize the sugar in the water in a heavy saucepan over low heat, swirling pan to prevent scorching. (You can use a wet pastry brush to wash down sugar crystals from the sides of the pan.) Cook at a low boil until medium brown. Stir in onions and pecans. Bring to a boil again over low heat until mixture reaches 250° on a candy thermometer. (Don't scorch.) Spread on a greased cookie sheet and cool completely before adding to ice cream.

*Don't attempt this recipe unless you can obtain the uniquely sweet, mild onions grown around Noonday. Even then, it's strange at best.

(continued on next page)

Cookoffs!

ICE CREAM
2¼ cups sugar
¼ cup plus 2 tablespoons flour
½ teaspoon salt
3 cups milk
1 12-ounce can evaporated milk
3 eggs
2 egg yolks
1 quart whipping cream
1 tablespoon vanilla

Combine sugar, flour, and salt in a 3-quart saucepan. Stir in milk and evaporated milk. Cook over medium heat until thickened, stirring constantly, about 15 minutes. Whisk eggs and yolks together. Slowly stir ¼ of custard into the eggs, then slowly return to saucepan so as not to curdle. Cook 1 more minute.

Chill, covered, in refrigerator for 2 hours. Combine cream and vanilla and add to cooled custard. Pour into ice-cream-freezer container and process until half set. Break up praline into small pieces and fold into ice cream. Continue freezing until firm. Pack ice over container and let cream ripen for 1 to 2 hours. Makes 1 gallon.

Diane Smotherman, Tyler

Indian Pudding
Potlatch, Carthage

½ cup molasses
¼ cup dark brown sugar
2 eggs
1 dash salt
¼ teaspoon baking soda
3 cups milk
1 cup yellow cornmeal
1 dash cinnamon
4 tablespoons butter, cut in small pieces
3 cups milk

Mix molasses, brown sugar, eggs, salt, baking soda, and 3 cups milk in a saucepan and bring to a boil. Slowly add cornmeal and cinnamon. When fully mixed and thick, stir in butter and 3 cups more milk. Pour into a well-oiled casserole and put the casserole into a larger pan of water. Bake at 300° for 1 hour. Lower heat to 275° and bake 6 more hours. Serves 8.

Carol Vincent, Carthage

Cinnamon Baked Bananas
Dutch Oven Cookoff, Terlingua

5 to 6 bananas
¼ cup butter
½ teaspoon vanilla (Mexican, if possible)
Cinnamon
Brown sugar
Slivered almonds
2 tablespoons rum or sotol (liquor made from sotol plant)

Peel bananas and slice lengthwise. Melt butter in Dutch oven with vanilla. Add bananas and sprinkle with cinnamon, sugar, almonds, and rum. Cover and bake over charcoal fire 20 minutes, with 5 coals under bottom, 6 on lid. Serves 5 to 6.

Tommy Davidson, Terlingua

Pecan Baklava
Winter Garden Pecan Bake Show, Hondo

ASSEMBLY
2 pounds butter, melted
2 pounds phyllo sheets
36 whole cloves

Brush a 12-by-18-by-2-inch baking pan with melted butter. Place 5 sheets of phyllo in the pan, brushing each with butter. Add one 9-ounce portion of nut filling and cover with 5 sheets of phyllo, brushing each with butter. Repeat the process until all the filling is used. Cover the top with 13 sheets of phyllo, brushed with butter. Score the top layer of phyllo diagonally in a diamond pattern to indicate 36 portions, each 3 by 2 inches. Insert a whole clove in each portion. Bake in a preheated 350° oven for 45 minutes. Remove from oven and immediately pour honey syrup over top of the baklava. Cool to room temperature and cut through the pastry where it is scored. Makes 3 dozen.

FILLING
1¼ pounds pecans, chopped
¾ pound almonds, sliced
1½ cups sugar
1 teaspoon cinnamon
1 teaspoon allspice

Combine ingredients in a large bowl. Divide into five 9-ounce portions and set aside.

(continued on next page)

Cookoffs!

SYRUP
2 cups sugar
1 cup water
1 cup honey
1 lemon, cut in half

Mix sugar, water, and honey in a saucepan. Bring to a boil. Add lemon halves, and boil until slightly thickened. Remove lemon and chill.

Sarah Moss, Hondo

Cinnamon Pecan Pull-apart Bread
Winter Garden Pecan Bake Show, Hondo

1 cup pecans, chopped
1 cup pecans, chopped
½ to 1 cup sugar
2 to 4 tablespoons cinnamon
2 loaves frozen bread dough, slightly thawed

Pour pecans in bottom of well-oiled funnel pan. Mix sugar and cinnamon together in a bowl. Melt margarine. Take bread dough and roll in golfball-size balls. Dip balls into melted margarine and then into cinnamon and sugar mixture. Place balls in 2 layers in the pan on top of pecans and let dough rise until double in volume. Bake at 350° for 30 minutes. Remove from oven and let cool for 10 minutes. Invert onto serving plate. Makes equivalent of 2 loaves.

Dana Cerney, Hondo.

Apple Pecan Kolaches
Fort Bend County Czech Fest, Rosenberg

DOUGH
2 packages dry yeast
½ cup warm milk (105°–115°)
⅓ cup sugar
½ cup butter, melted
½ cup warm milk (105°–115°)
⅓ cup sour cream
2 eggs, beaten
½ teaspoon salt
½ teaspoon vanilla
3½ to 4 cups flour
⅓ cup butter, melted

Combine milk and sugar and pour over yeast. Do not stir until yeast dissolves. Then stir and add remaining ingredients except last portion of melted butter. Mix well, adding flour a little at a time to make a soft dough. Cover and let rise for 30 minutes in a warm place. Stir and cover and let rise for another 30 minutes or until double in volume. Spoon onto floured surface and form into walnut-size balls. Put dough balls on buttered cookie sheets, flatten, and brush with the ⅓ cup melted butter. Make an indentation in the center of each, fill with fruit, and top with streusel. Let rise until almost double. Bake at 375° for about 20 minutes or until light brown. Glaze edges with thin mixture of powdered sugar and water while still warm. Makes 3 dozen.

FILLING

5 to 6 medium apples, peeled, pared, and finely chopped
1 teaspoon lemon juice
¾ cup sugar
2 tablespoons cornstarch
⅓ cup pecans, chopped
½ teaspoon vanilla

Put apples in a heavy, medium saucepan and stir in lemon juice. Mix sugar and cornstarch together and add to the apples. Stir well and cook over very low heat (be careful not to burn), stirring occasionally, until apples are tender, about 20 minutes. Add pecans and vanilla. Fill kolaches before baking.

Bernice Meyer, Richmond

Cottage Cheese Kolaches
Kolache Festival, Caldwell

DOUGH
2 packages dry yeast
½ cup warm water (105°–115°)
2 cups milk
4 tablespoons shortening
4 tablespoons sugar
2 teaspoons salt
6½ cups flour

Soften yeast in warm water. Scald milk; add shortening, sugar, and salt. Cool mixture until lukewarm and add yeast. Using an electric mixer or spoon, work in flour until you have a good dough and beat well. Put dough in a greased bowl, turn it to grease thoroughly, cover, and let rise until double in volume. Punch down and let rise again. When almost doubled the second time, roll out ½-inch thick and cut kolaches with a 2½-inch round cutter. Place kolaches in a greased pan and let them rise slightly. Then press indentations in the centers using your fingers or thumb and put some filling in each one. Let rise until almost double in volume. Bake at 350° for about 25 minutes. Add topping. Makes 4 dozen.

FILLING
6 ounces cottage cheese
1 tablespoon butter
2 tablespoons margarine, melted
1 egg yolk
1 cup sugar
1 tablespoon cornstarch
1 lemon, juice and grated rind

Mix together all ingredients except lemon and cook in a double boiler until thick and the right consistency for a filling. Remove from heat and add the lemon juice and rind. Cool. Place on kolache dough rounds before last rising.

TOPPING
Margarine, melted
8 ounces sour cream
Sugar

Brush each hot kolache with melted margarine. Drop a bit of sour cream in the center and spread. Sprinkle lightly with sugar.

Ella Drgac, Caldwell

Peach Kolaches
Kolache Festival, Caldwell

DOUGH
½ cup warm water (105°–115°)
¼ cup sugar
2 packages dry yeast or 2 cakes compressed yeast
1 cup lukewarm milk
2 eggs, beaten until foamy
6½ cups flour
½ cup vegetable oil
½ cup evaporated milk
1 teaspoon salt
⅓ cup sugar
½ cup margarine, melted

Mix water and ¼ cup sugar and pour over the yeast (if cake yeast is used, water should be 85°). Do not stir until after it foams (takes about 5 minutes). Mix milk with beaten eggs and add to yeast mixture. Add 2½ cups of the flour and mix well to make a soft dough. Let rise in a warm place for about 30 minutes. Add vegetable oil, evaporated milk, salt, and ⅓ cup sugar. Stir and then add remaining 4 cups flour. Work well with hands until dough is smooth. Cover with cloth or plastic wrap, put in a warm place, and let rise an inch or two.

Punch down and let rise again, until double in volume. Pinch off portions about the size of a walnut and press out about 2½ inches in diameter. Place individual kolaches in greased muffin pans or on a greased baking sheet. Flatten a little and brush with melted margarine. Make a small impression in the middle of each and top with peach filling. Or roll dough out as for cinnamon rolls. Spread with filling and roll in a cylinder and slice. Let rise in pans until slightly puffy, about 20 minutes. Bake in 400° oven until lightly browned, about 12 to 15 minutes. Makes 4 to 5 dozen.

Dough will also make 3 large fruit rolls; bake at 350° about 30 minutes.

PEACH FILLING
2 cups fresh peaches, peeled and sliced
⅔ cup sugar, or to taste
4 tablespoons flour
½ teaspoon cinnamon or nutmeg

Mix all ingredients and spoon on kolaches (or large fruit rolls) before baking.

Mary Siptak, Caldwell

Index

Allen, Reed, 108
Alligator logs, 86
Alpine, 66
Appetizers
  alligator logs, 86
  black-eyed pea wheels, 79
  chicken hors d'oeuvres olé, 84–85
  jalapeño jelly, 88
Apple pecan kolaches, 182–183
Archibald, Billy, 79
Armed Forces Annual Chili Cookoff, 55–56
Ashton Villa, 33–34
"Ashton Villa Vanilla" ice cream, 172
Athens: Black-Eyed Pea Jamboree, 3–4; Uncle Fletch Davis Memorial World Hamburger Cookoff, 4–6
Austin: Texas Ice Cream Crank-Off, 7–8

Bacon cornettes, 104
Baker, Rosa, 132
Baklava, 179–180
Bananas: baked, 178
Barbecue Cookoff, 63–64
Barbecue sauces, 128, 136–137
Barbecued chicken, 122, 128
Barbecued goat, 135–136
Barbecued lamb sauce, 137
Barbecued rabbit, 121
Barbecued shrimp, 134
Bassham, Carolyn, 35, 158
Bean Cookoff, 66
Beans: pinto, 94. See also Black-eyed peas
Bertram: Oatmeal Festival, 9–10, 148
Betancourt, Julian, 99
Big Spring: Chicken-Fried Steak World Championship, 11–12
Biscuit Cookoff, 66

Biscuits, 108. See also Breads
Black-Eyed Pea Jamboree, 3–4
Black-eyed pea wheels, 79
Black-eyed peas, 93
Bloom, Chuck, 91
Bonarrigo, Merrill, 15
Bonarrigo, Paul, 15
Borchardt, Ken, 129
Brady: Goat Cookoff, 13
Breads
  bacon cornettes, 104
  biscuits, 108
  cinnamon pecan pull-apart bread, 181
  cowboy crêpes, 109
  jalapeño hushpuppies, 106
  onion Italian bread, 97–98
  panocha bread, 99
  pumpernickel, 103
  rye bread, 102
  seafood hushpuppies, 105
  spicy hushpuppies, 107
  white bread, 100
  whole wheat bread, 101
Bryan: Messina Hof Winefest, 15

Cajun-style pinto beans, 94
Cake: cherry layer, 155–156
Caldwell: Kolache Festival, 17–18
Carthage: Potlatch, 19
Cedar Hut Gang, 136
Cerney, Dana, 181
Cherry layer cake, 155–156
Chesser, Barbara, 124
Chicken Cooking Contest, 73–74. See also Feather Fest
Chicken
  barbecued, 122, 128
  boursin, 125
  El Greco, 124
  fettuccine Southwest, 91
  hors d'oeuvres olé, 84–85
  lime roasted, 123

Cookoffs!

salad, 127
stew, 130–131
surprise, 129
Texas hot, 126
Chicken-fried steak, 141
Chicken-Fried Steak World
    Championship, 11–12
Chili
    cowgirl, 114
    Fast Eddie's, 113
    Jim Ivey's, 118
    north Texas red, 116
    "Old Snort, " 115
    Wes Ritchey's hat-pin, 117
Chili Cookoff
    Hereford, 37–38
    San Angelo, 55–56
    Terlingua, 67
Chilympiad, 57–58
Chiu, Loanne, 126
Chocolate ice cream, 174
Cinnamon baked bananas, 178
Cinnamon pecan pull-apart bread, 181
Clabaugh, Amy, 104
Cobbler, peach, 163
Cockrell, James A., 5
Coconut cream pie, 161
Coleman: Fiesta de la Paloma and Dove Cookoff, 21
Cook, Alison, 11
Cookie Chill-off, 65–66
Cookies
    corn flake macaroons, 167
    oatmeal crisps, 165
    pinwheels, 166
    skillet cookies, 168
Copperas Cove: Rabbit Fest, 23–24
Corn cookoff, 19
Corn flake macaroons, 167
Corn soup, 82
Cottage cheese kolaches, 184–185
Cotulla: La Salle County Wild

Hog Cookoff, 25
County fairs. See Gillespie County Fair
Cowboys, 27–28
Cowgirl Hall of Fame, 37–38
Creole fresh corn soup, 82
Crêpes, 109
Croom, Carolyn, 169
Czech Fest, 53–54. See also Kolache Festival

Daingerfield, 35
Davidson, Tommy, 178
Davis, Fletcher, 4–5
Denmon, Debra, 151
Desserts. See Cake; Cobbler; Cookies; Ice Cream; Kolaches; Pies; Pudding
Diamond, Ida, 171, 173–174
Diamond, Lou, 173–174
Dove Cookoff, 21
Dove: sweet and sour, 132
Drennan, Billy George, 92
Drgac, Ella, 17, 185
Duck with apricot rice, 133
Dutch Oven Cookoff, 66

Edinburg: Panocha Bread Cookoff, 27–28
Enchiladas, 147
Estes, Darlene, 147

Fairs. See Gillespie County Fair
Fajita Cookoff, 29–30
Fajitas
    description of, 75–76
    Fast Eddie's, 145
    outlaw, 144
    rum, 143
Fajitas Fandango, 66
Fast Eddie's, 76
Fast Eddie's chili, 113
Fast Eddie's fajitas, 145

Index

Feather Fest, 47. *See also* Chicken Cooking Contest
Fettuccine Southwest, 91
Fiesta de la Paloma and Dove Cookoff, 21
Folse, Parker, 105
Forestry Festival, 45
Forrest, Richard, 38, 114
Fort Bend County Czech Fest, 53–54
Fort Worth: Pioneer Days Fajita Cookoff, 29–30
Franco Villa Company, 85
Fredericksburg: Gillespie County Fair, 31–32, 167–168

Galveston: Ice Cream Crank-Off at Ashton Villa, 33–34
Gilbert, Barbara, 170
Gillespie County Fair, 31–32
Gilmer: Yamboree, 35–36
Goat: barbecued, 135–136
Goat Cookoff, 13
Goldman, Joanna, 81
Goodwin, Sharon, 148, 165
Green chili enchiladas, 147
Guinea gumbo, 151
Gumbo Cookoff, 51–52
Gumbo. *See also* Soups
 guinea, 151
 sausage and seafood, 150
 seafood, 149
Gutierrez, Miriam, 83

Hamburger Cookoff, 4–6
Hamburgers
 invention of, 4–5
 origin of name, 5
 recipe, 140
Hansel, John, 120
Harper, Margaret, 37
Herber, Dana, 156

Hereford: National Cowgirl Hall of Fame Chili Cookoff, 37–38
Hog: deep-fried wild, 139
Hog Cookoff, 25
Hondo: Winter Garden Pecan Bake Show, 39–40
Hopkins County Stew Cookoff, 61–62
Hors d'oeuvres. *See* Appetizers
Horton, Ezra, 13, 135
Horton, Ronnie, 13, 135
Hushpuppies
 jalapeño, 106
 seafood, 105
 spicy, 107
Hushpuppy Olympics, 45–46

Ice cream
 onion praline, 175–176
 pistachio fudge nut, 171
 praline, 175–176
 red-white-and-blueberry, 173
 strawberry cheesecake, 170
 Strawberry Riesling, 169
 "Texas Mud," 174
 vanilla, 172
Ice Cream Crank-Off, 7–8
Ice Cream Crank-Off at Ashton Villa, 33–34
Indian pudding, 177
Inman, Les, 43, 138
International Barbecue Cookoff, 63–64
International Gumbo Cookoff, 51–52
Ivey, Jim, 118

Jackson, Richard, 13, 135
Jalapeño Festival, 41–42
Jalapeño hushpuppies, 106
Jalapeño jelly, 88

Cookoffs!

Jalapeño and rice salad, 83
Jelly: jalapeño, 88
Jenschke, Jerome, 167–168
Jenschke, Mildred, 164

Key, Nell, 82
Kid, Jess, 151
King, Henrietta, 37
Knouse, David, 5, 140
Kolache Festival, 17–18. See also Czech Fest
Kolaches
　apple pecan, 182–183
　cottage cheese, 184–185
　peach, 186–187
Krenek, Carolyn, 162
Kutzer, Mike, 94, 143

La Salle County Wild Hog Cookoff, 25
LaFleur, Mrs. Ernest, 159
Laijas, Chuck, 87
Laijas, Megg, 87
Lajitas-on-the-Rio-Grande resort, 66
Lajitas Trading Post, 65, 66
Lamb: barbecued, 137
Lamblast, 56
Lane, Jim, 144
Laredo: Jalapeño Festival, 41–42
Leger, Dewayne, 86
Lime pie, 160
Lime roasted chicken, 123
Llano: Wild Game Cookoff, 43–44
Lufkin: Southern Hushpuppy Olympics, 45–46

Macaroons, 167
McDonald, Joan, 15, 157
McGaugh, Boyd, 106
Markow, Steve, 64
Massey, Louise, 37

Meats. See Chicken; Chicken-fried steak; Fajitas; Goat; Hamburgers; Hog; Lamb; Smothered steak
Messina Hof Winefest, 15
Meusebach, John O., 31
Meyer, Bernice, 183
Miller, Glenn, 46
Mitchell, Glenda, 131
Mohler, Bill, 55–56, 115
Mohler, Janie, 55, 115
Moore, Cathy, 166
Moss, Sarah, 180
Murchison, John, 4

National Cowgirl Hall of Fame Chili Cookoff, 37–38
Nixon: Feather Fest, 47
Noonday: Onion Festival, 49–50

Oatmeal crisps, 165
Oatmeal Festival, 9–10
Oatmeal quiche, 148
O'Daniel, W. Lee, 66
Onion Festival, 49–50
Onion Italian bread, 97–98
Onion praline ice cream, 175
Orange: International Gumbo Cookoff, 51–52

Pair, Tia, 127
Panocha bread, 99
Panocha Bread Cookoff, 27–28
Parks, Charlotte, 93
Pastas: fettuccine Southwest, 91
Pastries. See Pies
Pea-ta bread filled with zuc-pea-ni salad, 80–81
Peach cobbler, 163
Peach Jamboree, 59
Peach kolaches, 186–187

Index

Peach pie, 164
Peas. See Beans; Black-eyed peas
Pecan Bake Show, 39–40
Pecan baklava, 179–180
Pecan pie, 162
Petit, Kay, 142
Pies
  coconut cream, 161
  lime, 160
  peach, 164
  pecan, 162
  rum cream, 157
  strawberry rice, 159
  yam, 158
Pinto beans, 94
Pinwheels, 166
Pioneer Days Fajita Cookoff, 29–30
Pistachio fudge nut ice cream, 171
Pork. See Hog
Port Isabel, 76
Potatoes: campfire, 92
Potlatch, 19
Poultry. See Chicken
Praline ice cream, 175–176
Pudding: Indian, 177
Pumpernickel, 103

Quiche: oatmeal, 148

Rabbit: Szechwan, 120
Rabbit Fest, 23–24
Ranch-style smothered steak, 142
Red-white-and-blueberry ice cream, 173
Reed, Donna, 130
Republic of Texas Chilympiad, 57–58
Rice Festival, 71–72, 86
Rice
  chicken salad, 127
  duckling with apricot rice, 133
  jalapeño and rice salad, 83
  strawberry rice pie, 159
Ritchey, Wes, 117
Robbins, Harold, 57
Rosenberg: Fort Bend County Czech Fest, 53–54
Rum cream pie, 157
Rum fajitas, 143
Rye bread, 102

Salads
  chicken salad, 127
  jalapeño and rice salad, 83
  pea-ta bread with zuc-pea-ni salad, 80–81
San Angelo: Armed Forces Annual Chili Cookoff, 55–56; Lamblast, 56
San Marcos: Republic of Texas Chilympiad, 57–58
Sauces. See Barbecue sauces
Sausage and seafood combination gumbo, 150
Scheffield, Marge, 172
Schmidt, David, 134
Seafood gumbo, 149–150
Seafood hushpuppies, 105
Shobe, Glenda, 109
Shrimp: barbecued, 134
Siptak, Mary, 17, 187
Skillet cookies, 168
Smith, "Chicken Martha," 122
Smothered steak, 142
Smotherman, Diane, 49–50, 98, 176
Soups. See also Gumbo
  corn, 82
  tortilla, 87
Southern Hushpuppy Olympics, 45–46
Sparkman, Nell, 130
Station KOOV, 121
Steak. See Chicken-fried steak; Smothered steak
Stew Cookoff, 61–62
Stews: chicken, 130–131
Stonewall: Peach Jamboree,

Cookoffs!

59
Strawberry cheesecake ice cream, 170
Strawberry rice pie, 159
Strawberry riesling ice cream, 169
Stubenrauch, Joseph W., 59
Sulphur Springs: Hopkins County Stew Cookoff, 61–62
Sweet potatoes. See Yam pie
Sweet-and-sour dove, 132
Szechwan rabbit, 120

Talamantez, Ben, 87
Talamantez, Nancy, 87
Talburt, Hollis F., 123
Talley, Beverly, 129
Tamale and corn fiesta, 146
Taylor: International Barbecue Cookoff, 63–64
Terlingua
  Bean Cookoff, 66
  Cookie Chill-Off, 65–66
  Dutch Oven Cookoff, 66
  Fajitas Fandango, 66
  W. Lee "Pappy" O'Daniel Biscuit Cookoff, 66
  World Championship Chili Cookoff, 67
Texas Chicken Cooking Contest, 73–74, 123–126
Texas Ice Cream Crank-Off, 7–8
"Texas Mud" ice cream, 174
Texas Ranch Roundup Cookoff, 69–70
Texas Rice Festival, 71–72, 86
Tiller, Jonaid, 139
Tolbert, Frank X., 4, 6, 57
Tolbert's Texas Chili Parlor, 5–6, 140
Tortilla soup, 87
"Touch of the Tropics" chicken salad, 127
Tyler, 49

Tyler, Linda, 57–58
Tyler, Tom, 57, 116

Uncle Fletch Davis Memorial World Hamburger Cookoff, 4–6

Vanilla ice cream, 172
Vegetables
  black-eyed peas, 93
  campfire potatoes, 92
  pinto beans, 94
Venable, Billie, 125
Vincent, Carol, 177
Vincent, David, 128

W. Lee "Pappy" O'Daniel Biscuit Cookoff, 66
Walters, Polly, 131
Washington's Birthday Festival, 41
Webb-Miller, Mimi, 160
Weinheimer, DeAnn, 163
Wells, R. J., 150
Whatley, Kriste, 133
White bread, 100
Whitley, Ern, 137
Whole wheat bread, 101
Wichita Falls: Texas Ranch Roundup Cookoff, 69–70
Wild game. See Dove; Hog; Rabbit
Wild Game Cookoff, 43–44
Wild Hog Cookoff, 25
Winefest, 15
Winnie: Texas Rice Festival, 71–72, 86
Winter Garden Pecan Bake Show, 39–40
Woods, Dianne, 161
Woodward, Dick, 140
Woodward Ranch, 66
World Championship Chili

Index

Cookoff, 67
Worrell, Ursula, 100–103
Wright, O.O., 46, 107
Wrinkle, Dave, 12, 141

Yam pie, 158
Yamboree, 35–36
Young, Juanita, 149